Randall Balmer

SAVING FAITH

How American Christianity Can
Reclaim Its Prophetic Voice

Fortress Press
Minneapolis

SAVING FAITH
How American Christianity Can Reclaim Its Prophetic Voice

Copyright © 2023 by Randall Balmer. Published by Fortress Press, an imprint of 1517 Media. All rights reserved. Except for brief quotations in critical articles or reviews, no part of this book may be reproduced in any manner without prior written permission from the publisher. Email copyright@1517.media or write to Permissions, Fortress Press, PO Box 1209, Minneapolis, MN 55440-1209.

Scripture quotations marked (NIV) are taken from the Holy Bible, New International Version®, NIV®. Copyright © 1973, 1978, 1984, 2011 by Biblica, Inc.™ Used by permission of Zondervan. All rights reserved worldwide. www.zondervan.com. The "NIV" and "New International Version" are trademarks registered in the United States Patent and Trademark Office by Biblica, Inc.™

Library of Congress Control Number: 2023933063 (print)

Cover image: Abstract Oil Painting Smudged Textured Brush Strokes, ©oxygen | Getty Images
Cover design: Kristin Miller

Print ISBN: 978-1-5064-8806-6
eBook ISBN: 978-1-5064-8807-3

Printed in China.

ALSO BY RANDALL BALMER

Mine Eyes Have Seen the Glory: A Journey into the Evangelical Subculture in America

A Perfect Babel of Confusion: Dutch Religion and English Culture in the Middle Colonies

For Douglas Frank and Sam Alvord
who introduced me to the life of the mind
and the music of the spheres

We all, like sheep, have gone astray, each of us has turned to our own way.

—Isaiah 53:6

I can see no reason, but the most deceitful one, for calling the religion of this land Christianity. I look upon it as the climax of all misnomers, the boldest of all frauds and the grossest of all libels.

—Frederick Douglass, 1845

It is customary to blame secularism for the eclipse of religion in modern society. But it would be more honest to blame religion for its own defeats. Religion declined not because it was refuted, but because it became irrelevant, dull, oppressive and insipid. When faith becomes an heirloom rather than a living fountain, when religion speaks only in the name of authority rather than with the voice of compassion—its message becomes meaningless.

—Abraham Joshua Heschel, 1976

. . . there is an enormous number of people, and I am one of them, whose native religion, for better or worse, is Christianity. We were born to it; we began to learn about it before we became conscious; it is, whatever we think of it, an intimate belonging of our being; it informs our consciousness, our language, and our dreams.

We can turn away from it or against it, but that will only bind us tightly to a reduced version of it. A better possibility is that this, our native religion, should survive and renew itself, so that it may become as largely and truly instructive as we need it to be.

—Wendell Berry, 1993

CONTENTS

PREFACE

Anyone who sifts through the ashes of American Christianity in the early decades of the twenty-first century owes his readers the clarity of knowing who presumes to do so.

I identify myself as a follower of Jesus, even though I'm acutely aware that I often fall short of that aspiration. It's well beyond my pay grade to assert that my faith is necessarily superior to others'; that discussion holds little interest for me. I've examined other traditions from time to time, and I've come away with appreciation for their integrity, but those traditions are not mine, and I seek fully to inhabit my own faith, Christianity.

Specifically, I grew up in the evangelical subculture in the middle decades of the twentieth century. My father was a minister for more than four decades in the Evangelical Free Church of America, and I honor both his ministry and his memory. I "accepted Jesus into my heart" at an early age (and many times thereafter). I attended Sunday school, vacation Bible school, and Bible camp, and my evangelical formation culminated in a baccalaureate degree from Trinity College, in Deerfield, Illinois, and a master's degree from its sister institution, Trinity Evangelical Divinity School. In short, I'll put my credentials as an evangelical up against anyone—including Franklin Graham, by the way, although I concede that his father, Billy Graham, might have been a bit more famous than mine.

It's fair to say that I drifted away from evangelicalism during graduate school, but not because of rejection or rebellion. I simply found that I was no longer interested in the pitched, vicious, internecine battles over such issues as biblical inerrancy that I had witnessed in seminary. I had focused my doctoral studies and my dissertation on religion in colonial America, but while teaching at Columbia University in the late 1980s the televangelist scandals broke—Jim and Tammy Faye Bakker, Oral Roberts, Jimmy Swaggart—and the media began asking about evangelicals and evangelicalism. Although I was happy to respond to their queries, I quickly tired of the assumption that all evangelicals were either gullible or the moral equivalent of Swaggart or Jim Bakker. Having grown up in that world, I knew better, so I resolved to write a kind of travelogue about evangelicals at the grassroots, a book entitled *Mine Eyes Have Seen the Glory: A Journey into the Evangelical Subculture in America.*

By the time I returned to evangelicalism late in the 1980s, however, I found elements of the subculture I could no longer recognize. White evangelicalism by that time had merged with the far-right precincts of the Republican Party in a movement known as the Religious Right. (I find the term

"Christian Right" deeply offensive; there's precious little that I can identify as *Christian* about it.)

Which brings me to the current project. The religion of my childhood, the kindness and the compassion that I witnessed in my parents, had become coarse and tendentious and yes, hateful. Far too many evangelical leaders lusted after political power and cultural influence, and they were prepared to sacrifice any remaining principles they once possessed in order to secure it. Other expressions of the Christian faith, specifically mainline Protestantism and Roman Catholicism, were not much more attractive, for reasons that I will outline presently.

This book is not about me, although my background and my experience inevitably inform my analysis. Nevertheless, allow me to advance the narrative far enough to say that my spiritual pilgrimage led me to the Episcopal Church. I was ordained a priest in 2006 and served as rector of two parishes coincident with my teaching and research. I have also served as a supply priest in Connecticut, New Hampshire, Vermont, and New Mexico.

Whether or not I still identify as an evangelical requires a longer conversation and a careful definition of terms to bracket out the distortions of the Religious Right. As the following pages will demonstrate, however, I care deeply about the integrity of the Christian faith.

❦ 1 ❧

HOW BAD IS IT?

. . . all our righteous acts are like filthy rags

—Isaiah 64:6

ALTHOUGH BOTH THE evidence and the explanations are contested, few Americans would question the assertion that Christianity is facing something of a crisis these days. Although megachurches continue to be visible on the American religious landscape, more menacing than ever to many Americans, some evangelicals are leaving the fold, fed up with the leaders and the direction of the movement. Mainline Protestants are splitting over sexual identity issues and facing a demographic crisis in the form of aging congregants, and the Roman Catholic hierarchy faces a credibility crisis with the lingering effects of the pedophilia scandals.

Explanations vary for the crisis in American Christianity. One camp insists that secularization is the root of the problem, increasingly constricting expressions of faith in the public arena. Christians, in this view, are embattled, their morality held up to ridicule in popular culture, their beliefs brushed aside as superstition, their children subjected to all manner of indoctrination in schools and in the media. Such a situation calls for vigilance and pushing back against the tides of secularism in society by any means necessary, including legislation, judicial action, even vigilantism.

Another view agrees that Christianity is on the ropes in American life, but the fault lies with Christians themselves. For too long Christianity has exerted a hegemonic grip on society—a majority of Americans identify as Christians, after all—and they have imposed their will on other religious traditions, or those with no religion whatsoever. Why should IN GOD WE TRUST be emblazoned on our coins and currency, they ask, or why should "under God" be inserted into the Pledge of Allegiance? This is not a Christian nation; the First Amendment mandated no religious establishment. Besides, the behavior of these so-called Christians—the hatred, the racism, the intolerance—hardly qualifies as godly. As Mohandas Gandhi famously observed, "I like your Christ, I do not like your Christians. Your Christians are so unlike your Christ." The demise of Christianity, in this view, is warranted: If Christians cannot learn to behave in a multicultural society, to play well with others, they deserve to diminish in numbers and influence.

Both arguments have merit, and both sides feel aggrieved. What is incontestable, however, is that Christianity, although its grip on society is still formidable, no longer has the influence in American life that it once had.

Numbers don't tell the whole story, but let's start there. According to the Pew Research Center, 63 percent of Americans identified as Christian in 2021. That's a high percentage, one that eclipses other Western nations, but it represents a drop from 75 percent a decade earlier. Correspondingly, 19 percent of Americans identified as "atheist, agnostic or no particular faith" in 2011; ten years later the number of "nones" rose ten percentage points to 29 percent. "The secularizing shifts evident in American society so far in the 21st century show no signs of slowing," according to the report. "The religiously unaffiliated share of the public is 6 percentage points higher than it was five years ago and 10 points higher than a decade ago."[1]

If we delve more deeply into the survey results, it becomes clear that the drop-off is not merely a matter of shedding religious affiliations. In a fourteen-year span between 2007 and 2021, the percentage of Americans who say that religion is "very important" in their lives fell from 56 percent to 41 percent; in 2021, 45 percent of Americans said they prayed daily, down from 58 percent in 2007.[2]

Once again, the blame game spins into high gear. One explanation holds that the cancer of unrelenting, unchecked secularism has eroded religious belief, so it should not be surprising that faith is waning. Another view asserts that now, into the fifth decade of the Religious Right's alliance with the far-right reaches of the Republican Party, Christianity has been so tainted by that association that many Americans choose simply to sever ties with Christianity itself for fear of being associated with politics they regard as repugnant. "Many people turning away from religion do so because they think of religion as an expression of political conservatism or as a wing of the Republican Party," according to David Campbell of the University of Notre Dame. "The more religion is wrapped up in a political view, the more people who don't share that political view say, 'That's not for me.'"[3]

Despite the tendency of some groups, especially evangelicals and Roman Catholics, to consider only themselves and their fellow believers as "Christians," the label applies to a variety of traditions, everything from Eastern Orthodoxy to the Black church, from evangelicalism and mainline Protestantism to Roman Catholicism. In addition, Jehovah's Witnesses and the Latter-day Saints claim the mantle "Christian," even though other Christians remain chary about granting that designation.

If we take the three largest Christian groups in the Pew survey—Mainline Protestant (14.7 percent), Evangelical Protestant (25.4 percent), and Roman Catholic (20.8 percent)—and look more closely at their recent history, we can more easily understand how Christianity is losing credibility in American society.

Mainline Protestantism is a term that refers generally to older, more established Protestant denominations: Lutherans, Methodists, Disciples of Christ, Presbyterians, Congregationalists, the Episcopal Church. In the aggregate, mainline

Protestantism has been hemorrhaging in all three indices of attendance, membership, and giving since the mid-1960s. The reasons are numerous, complex, and once again, contested. Without any doubt, demographics play a role. Mainline Protestants skew older, in part because when these denominations began to face financial stringencies in the 1960s, one of the first budget items they cut was funds for campus ministry. That, coupled with the antiestablishment and anti-institutional mood of the counterculture, made mainline Protestantism less attractive to a younger generation. In addition, as David A. Hollinger demonstrates, mainline Protestants "supported an expanded role for women, approved a role for sex other than procreation, and encouraged the use of contraceptives." This led to lower birth rates relative to evangelicals, who were much slower to embrace these ideas.[4]

Demographics of a different sort also figure into this history. Many of these mainline congregations had invested a great deal of capital into magnificent, architecturally distinguished churches in downtown locations. With the post-World War II flight to the suburbs, these congregations faced a difficult choice: Do they abandon their physical plants and follow their congregants to the suburbs, or do they take a principled decision to remain in the city? I remember very clearly when I was writing a profile of First United Methodist Church in Orlando, Florida, for *Christian Century* in 1990. That congregation had elected to remain downtown, but the price for doing so was a radical downsizing of their programs and staff from the glory days of the 1950s. As congregants, overwhelmingly white, fled to the suburbs, they became increasingly reluctant to venture back into the city, especially as parking became more and more scarce.[5]

David Hollinger also argues that, contrary to accepted wisdom, mainline Protestantism became more demanding of its congregants during this era. While white evangelicals hunkered into the largely homogenous world of Norman Rockwell-style nostalgia, mainline leaders challenged their followers to adjust to a racially diverse, scientifically informed society. In so doing, mainline Protestantism began to lose influence because some of the people in the pews resented and resisted those demands. The general support of these leaders for the civil rights movement and their opposition to the war in Vietnam during the 1960s, moreover, clashed with the views of many mainline Protestants in local congregations, who felt ostracized from denominational hierarchies. At the same time that conservatives were drifting toward evangelicalism, progressive Protestants concerned about race, gender, sexuality, and empire complained that mainline Protestantism was too slow to adopt liberal ideas; these progressives gravitated away from the church and embraced secular activism.[6]

Both symbolically and intentionally, leaders of mainline denominations clustered themselves in proximity to one another in the Interchurch Center on the Upper West Side of Manhattan, far away from grassroots Protestants. In 1950, when the National Council of Churches announced plans to construct the Interchurch Center, many Protestant believers objected to the insularity of the location; one letter to *Christian Century* suggested Emporia or Manhattan, Kansas, as a more appropriate venue than Manhattan, New York City, if denominational executives truly cared about maintaining ties with their congregants at the grassroots.[7]

Finally, mainline Protestantism has been hobbled in recent years by a fixation with ecumenism, the notion that Christian groups should elide denominational and theological differences in the name of Christian unity. Although this is not the place to rehearse the arguments, I have deep reservations about the theological justifications for and the utility of ecumenism, but the undeniable fact is that an emphasis on ecumenism has tended to produce an ideology of the lowest common denominator, one almost entirely innocent of historical context or theological ballast. As a student of religion in North America, I'm well aware of the history and the theological roots of various Protestant denominations, but those distinguishing features have been all but obliterated in the rush toward ecumenism.[8]

The concomitant emphasis on inclusion within mainline Protestantism—gender equality, racial inclusion, the embrace of various sexual identities—has had the paradoxical effect of driving many Christians away from mainline Protestantism. My sense as a historian of American religion is that the most successful religious movements in American history have been *exclusive*, rather than *inclusive*. The Methodists and the Mormons of the nineteenth century come to mind, as well as the evangelicals of the twentieth century or Roman Catholicism throughout American history. These movements have clear boundaries and well-defined beliefs, and many associated with those groups have rarely been shy about characterizing mainline Protestantism as something akin to a miasma of theological mush.

Remember those mainline Protestants who decamped to the suburbs following World War II? As they settled into their new environs and grew increasingly reluctant to venture back into the city to attend church, they began looking for alternatives closer to home. And who was waiting for them? More likely than not, an evangelical church of one stripe or another was there, offering amenities ranging from childcare and recreation to youth programs and copious, no-hassle parking.

The great genius of evangelicalism throughout American history has been the ability of evangelicals to speak the idiom of the culture, whether it be the open-air preaching of George Whitefield in the eighteenth century, the circuit riders and the colporteurs of the nineteenth century, the urban evangelism of Billy Sunday and Billy Graham in the twentieth century, or the suburban, shopping-mall-style megachurches of more recent vintage. In part because of the absence of denominational hierarchies or the constraints of liturgy or tradition, evangelical churches are constantly experimenting with new approaches, fresh strategies for attracting and keeping audiences. The "praise music" craze provides one example.

Originating with the Jesus movement of the early 1970s in southern California, this participatory musical genre with its soft, lilting, simple melodies has almost universally replaced classic hymnals in evangelical worship—whereas mainline Protestants generally cling to their hymnals.

The radically decentralized nature of evangelicalism—evangelicals typically are not bound by liturgy, creeds, hierarchy, or tradition—leaves it susceptible to the cult of personality and the concomitant dangers of authoritarianism. Charismatic individuals galvanize followers into congregations and, through media, larger audiences. Especially among groups with no denominational affiliation, however, this often leads to a lack of accountability. The televangelist scandals of the late 1980s provide perhaps the best example, but more recent controversies around abuses of authority and sexual misbehavior have rocked such organizations as Mars Hill Church in Seattle, Ravi Zacharias International Ministries, Kanakuk Kamps, Willow Creek Community Church in Illinois, Bill Gothard's Institute in Basic Life Principles, *Christianity Today* magazine, and the Southern Baptist Convention, among others. The popularity and apparent success of leaders of these organizations, together with the absence of accountability structures, shielded their reprehensible actions from public scrutiny, at least for a time.

In recent decades, this evangelical populism has been redirected toward political ends. Although white evangelicals were largely apolitical throughout the middle decades of the twentieth century, and they certainly were not organized politically, that began to change during the 1970s. The initial catalyst was Jimmy Carter's campaign for the presidency. Carter, a "born again" Southern Baptist Sunday school teacher, spoke unabashedly about his faith, and his emphasis on decency and honesty, especially in the wake of the Watergate scandal, propelled him to the White House. Paradoxically, many of the same evangelicals who elected Carter in 1976, some for the simple novelty of voting for one of their own, turned dramatically against him four years later.

The genesis of their political mobilization in the 1970s goes a long way toward explaining evangelicals' diminished moral authority in the early decades of the twenty-first century. Despite a decades-long campaign to persuade Americans that the Religious Right galvanized as a political movement in response to the Supreme Court's 1973 *Roe v. Wade* decision, the historical record provides no support whatsoever for that assertion. Evangelicals considered abortion a "Catholic issue" throughout the 1970s, and in fact several evangelical leaders applauded the *Roe* decision—while most said nothing at all. The catalyst for evangelical political mobilization in the 1970s was the defense of racial discrimination in evangelical institutions, including Bob Jones University. Only much later, on the eve of the 1980 presidential election, did the leaders of the Religious Right "discover" abortion as a political issue. That discovery, in turn, was a godsend, because it allowed leaders of the Religious Right to divert attention from the real origins of their movement.[9]

So, what should we make of this information? What difference does it make that the genesis of the Religious Right lay in the defense of racial segregation—or, in a word, racism? Jesus enjoined his followers to judge a tree by its fruit, so I think it's appropriate to trace the history of the Religious Right from its roots in racism to the 2016 presidential election, when 81 percent of white evangelicals supported Donald Trump, a self-confessed sexual predator and decidedly not a champion of the "family values" that the Religious Right claimed to be upholding for the previous three-plus decades.

My sense as a historian is that unacknowledged and unrepented racism tends to fester, and the persistent attempts to peddle the "abortion myth" forestalled white evangelicals' reckoning with the racism embedded into the Religious Right; the leaders of the movement pulled off a classic bait and switch. Nor was support for Donald Trump the first evidence of lingering racism. Until recently, the Religious Right's embrace of Ronald Reagan over Carter in 1980 had long mystified me. Why would evangelicals reject one of their own, a "born again" Sunday school teacher, in favor of a divorced and remarried former actor from Hollywood, a province not known to evangelicals for its piety? Reagan, moreover, as governor of California had signed into law the most liberal abortion bill in the country.

Having written a biography of Carter, I'm well aware of the turbulence he faced as he headed into his reelection campaign—a sour economy, runaway inflation, renewed Soviet imperial ambitions, the taking of American hostages in Iran—and I don't deny the importance of those factors. It was not easy being president in the late 1970s, especially in the wake of the Arab Oil Embargo, which disrupted not only the economy but everyday life for millions of Americans. And despite Carter's missteps, I'm still not persuaded that anyone could have handled the situation appreciably better.[10]

Still, the logic of the Religious Right's support for Reagan, whom evangelicals came to regard as a political messiah, had long eluded me. Trump's evident racism—his caricature of immigrants, his description of "shithole countries," his embrace of "birtherism," his praise for white supremacists—and the approbation he nevertheless received from white evangelicals, provided a clue, and I began to review more closely Reagan's rhetoric and his political career.[11]

Reagan entered California politics in opposition to the Rumford Fair Housing Act, which sought to ensure equal access both to the rental and the purchase of property. He was an outspoken opponent of both the Civil Rights Act of 1964 and the Voting Rights Act of 1965. Throughout his political campaigns, he frequently invoked the racially charged slogan "law and order," and who can forget his vile caricature of mythical "welfare queens," women of color who supposedly lived lives of luxury on the public dole? Reagan was never able to produce one of these "welfare queens," but he sounded certain that they existed.

Aside from Reagan's decimation of the Civil Rights Commission as president and his consistent support for the apartheid regime in South Africa, the most compelling demonstration of his sentiments on race occurred at the Neshoba County Fair, in Philadelphia, Mississippi, on August 3, 1980. It was there that Reagan chose to open his general election campaign for the presidency—not somewhere in the Rust Belt to call attention to economic distress or even in his adopted home of California, then considered a swing state. No. Reagan chose Philadelphia, Mississippi, the place where, sixteen summers earlier, members of the Ku Klux Klan in collusion with the local sheriff's office abducted, tortured, and murdered three civil rights workers. Reagan was the master of symbolism, but lest anyone miss his meaning on that occasion at the Neshoba County Fair, he invoked the age-old segregationist battle cry, "I believe in states' rights."

The line from the origins of the Religious Right in defense of racism, then, to Donald Trump lassoes some rather unsavory characters: Roy S. Moore, for example, the "Ten Commandments Judge" in Alabama who praised the days of slavery as a "time when families were united," or Tony Perkins, head of the Family Research Council, who has had repeated dealings with the Ku Klux Klan and the White Citizens' Council, known colloquially as the "uptown Klan." But that line of connection between the genesis of the Religious Right and Trump also loops through the political career of Ronald

Reagan, the man still considered something of a demigod by many white evangelicals.[12]

If mainline Protestantism has effectively marginalized itself, and white evangelicals have yet to confront the crucible of racism, the third major Christian tradition in America, Roman Catholicism, carries its own historical baggage, which compromises its moral authority. I suppose I could dispense with the topic with one word, *pedophilia*, but I think the moral crisis besetting American Catholicism goes beyond that.

Priestly pedophilia is a tragedy on so many levels: the loss of credibility for the church and its clergy, financial hardship, and most of all its devastating effects on victims themselves and their families. Human frailty being what it is, we should not be surprised that abuse happens, catastrophic and regrettable though it may be. But the Catholic hierarchy compounded the damage by promising to address the situation internally rather than submit the matter to police and civil authorities. John Paul II was a charismatic figure, admired both by Catholics and non-Catholics, but his refusal adequately to confront the pedophilia crisis (compounded by the failure of his successor, Benedict XVI) represents a blot on the papacy.

The Catholic hierarchy essentially approached the issue by reasserting the great medieval synthesis (though not in so many words), a reference to a time when the Vatican sought to elevate its claims of authority over all other temporal powers. The best historical example is the so-called Investiture

Controversy, when in 1077 Pope Gregory VII kept the Holy Roman Emperor, Henry IV, kneeling outside in the snow for three days, awaiting a papal blessing.

In the case of priestly pedophilia, the posture of the hierarchy was, "We'll take care of our own affairs and handle this internally." The Roman Catholic Church spectacularly failed to do so. Instead, in far too many instances pedophile priests, rather than face prosecution, were quietly reassigned to different parishes or other positions of pastoral responsibility, places where they were once again in the position to abuse children ostensibly under their spiritual care. The pedophilia scandal reached into the highest levels of church hierarchy in the United States, notably Bernard Law and Theodore McCarrick, both of whom had held the titles of archbishop and cardinal.

Given the tragic comeuppance of McCarrick and Law, as well as the church's shameful handling of the whole matter, it would be logical to think that the Catholic hierarchy in the United States, its credibility very much in question, might be careful about issuing ethical pronouncements. Well, no. The United States Conference of Catholic Bishops instead has taken on the mantle of moral policeman in political matters.

Following the election of only the second Roman Catholic as president of the United States in 2020, the head of the Conference of Catholic Bishops, José Gomez, archbishop of Los Angeles, declared that Joseph Biden's support for abortion rights presented the church with a "difficult and complex situation." The conference then proceeded to debate whether to deny the president access to Holy Communion, the body and blood of Christ, much the way that conservative bishops ruled that John Kerry, the Democratic presidential nominee in 2004, would not be welcome at the communion rail.[13]

This same Conference of Catholic Bishops had rushed to congratulate Donald Trump after his victory in 2016, even before the results were certified. In 2020, however, at least one member of the conference, Joseph Strickland, of Tyler, Texas, refused to acknowledge Biden's victory.

To try even to pretend that there is anything approaching moral equivalency between Joe Biden and Donald Trump, let alone to decide the matter in Trump's favor, represents an appalling failure to exercise ethical judgment and another reason that the Catholic Church faces a credibility crisis. In what moral universe is it preferable to favor a political figure who separated refugee children from their parents and confined them to cages, who bore false witness more than thirty thousand times during the course of his presidency, and whose personal life is littered with divorces and extramarital affairs—in what moral universe is that man preferable to a lifelong devout Roman Catholic, a public servant who happens to believe, on the basis of constitutional principles and Supreme Court precedent, that the painful choice to terminate a pregnancy should be determined by the mother herself and not by the state?

The election of only the second Roman Catholic as president of the United States—and one who, by the way, is much more devout than the first—should prompt a call for unity among Catholics themselves, but also for all Americans. Instead, some bishops sought to deny Biden the body and blood of Christ.

The era of the great medieval synthesis is long past. The Catholic bishops have every right to offer moral guidance, although the faithful might want seriously to consider the provenance of that guidance. But the bishops have no right—or, in my judgment, moral standing—to bully a public official, even a member of their church, especially when their own credibility is suspect.

With the demise of mainline Protestantism, the unrepented racism of the Religious Right, and the moral credibility of the Roman Catholic Church in question, is it any wonder that Christianity in America is in decline?

2

MISGUIDED REMEDIES

Do not conform to the pattern of this world, but be transformed by the renewing of your mind.

—Romans 12:2

THE FOLLOWERS OF a religious tradition that has enjoyed near hegemonic status for centuries might be excused for trying to claw back their influence in a changing, multicultural society. One of the most tempting strategies for doing so is nostalgia, and it works something like this: Remember when our values were ascendant, when families were intact, when everyone went to church, when crime was nonexistent, when men were men and women were women?

It's a powerful appeal, and it has been invoked countless times, often coupled with rhetoric about traditional or "family values." Especially in the early years of the Religious Right, the focus of this earlier idyllic age was the 1950s and early 1960s, before the civil rights movement, the sexual revolution, and the counterculture. On more than a few occasions, conservative leaders invoked television programs of that era—*Father Knows Best* or the *Andy Griffith Show* or *Leave It to Beaver*—as examples of a happier time when society was ordered, and everyone was (or so it seemed) blissfully happy.

The lure of Mayberry is strong, and Mount Airy, North Carolina, which is Andy Griffith's hometown and claims to be the inspiration for the *Andy Griffith Show*, attracts thousands and thousands of visitors each year. In a 2021 segment for *CBS Sunday Morning*, Ted Koppel visited Mount Airy and talked with the tourists. A woman from Ohio described the *Andy Griffith Show* as "Good, clean comedy. Moral values. You don't find that a lot today." Another man explained the attraction of Mayberry. "The godless society that we see today," he said, "is longing for a simple life."[1]

But the past, especially as viewed through the sepia lens of nostalgia and memory, can be deceiving. Yes, many white middle-class families enjoyed comfortable lives, upward mobility, and relatively stable households in post-World War II America. But that veneer of family stability relied on the fact that many women were not pursuing careers or working outside the home, and people of color decidedly did not participate fully in the postwar prosperity available to white citizens. America in the 1950s, especially before the civil rights movement, was a two-tiered society, white and nonwhite; in the *Andy Griffith Show*'s eight seasons, for example, only one African American had a speaking part. And this summary does not even begin to account for the fact that many Americans led clandestine lives, fearful of being outed to family, friends, or employers because of their sexual identity.

Still, the yearning for a halcyon past is powerful, and the decade of the 1960s and early 1970s merely deepened the sense that Christians and Christianity were losing influence. The FDA's approval of the birth-control pill on May 9, 1960, launched the sexual revolution in the 1960s, and two Supreme Court decisions in the early 1960s held that Bible reading and prescribed prayer in public schools violated the establishment clause of the First Amendment. The anti-Vietnam protests; the urban riots in Detroit, Los Angeles, and Newark; and the assassinations of John F. Kennedy, Medgar Evers, Malcolm X, Martin Luther King Jr., and Robert Kennedy contributed to a sense that society was careening out of control.

Arguably the most consequential change in American society, the one with the most profound and lasting repercussions, attracted little notice at the time. On October 3, 1965, Lyndon B. Johnson signed the Hart–Celler Act on Liberty Island in New York Harbor. The bill, also known as the Immigration and Nationality Act of 1965, abolished the highly restrictive immigration quotas established by Congress in 1924 and opened the way for immigrants, especially from Asia and Africa. As these immigrants, many of them professionals, came to the United States in the ensuing decades, they began to change the complexion of America (quite literally), as well as the composition of American religions.

Many of these religions had been present in America for decades, especially following the World's Parliament of Religions in Chicago in 1893, but over time the Hart–Celler

Act admitted to the United States a critical mass of practitioners. As a consequence, and over the years, they altered the religious landscape of the United States with the appearance of Hindu temples, Shintō shrines, Islamic mosques, Sikh gurdwārās, or Buddhist stupas—some of them in unlikely places.

Sadly, many Christians regard this development as a zero-sum game: Any increase in "world religions," they fear, comes at the cost of Christian hegemony. While there is certainly some truth to that argument—expanding the range of choices in the buffet of religion in America diminishes the likelihood that "consumers" will choose Christianity— it misses the point about the positive effects of competition among religions. First, at least until recently Christianity has rarely suffered in the marketplace of religious ideas. In addition, America's best idea is the First Amendment, which simultaneously guaranteed freedom of religious expression and prohibited the legal establishment of any one religion. This was a radical notion at the time of the nation's founding, but the founders recognized the perils of state-favored religion and understood religious coercion as a species of tyranny.

The First Amendment, with its proscription on religious establishment, set up a free market of religion in the United States, where no tradition enjoys privileged status or tax revenues from the state. All compete on an equal footing, and the consequence of what one historian has called this "lively experiment" has been a vibrant, salubrious religious culture. Religious entrepreneurs, to extend the economic metaphor, compete with one another for popular followings, thereby lending an energy and dynamism to religion in America unmatched anywhere in the world.[2]

One of the characteristics of religion in colonial America, and one that bedeviled any attempts to designate one faith as the state religion, was the range of religious expressions. If we charted the religious affiliations of the Atlantic colonies in the seventeenth century, we would find an astonishing variety. Puritanism was ascendent in New England, although the Pilgrims (who had earlier separated from the Church of England) claimed what is now the eastern part of Massachusetts. Roger Williams, founder of the Baptist tradition in America, ensured that Rhode Island would be a haven for religious freedom. New Netherland was colonized by the Dutch West India Company, and the earliest European religious influence was the Dutch Reformed Church, although the colony very quickly included other religious groups: Quakers, Puritans, Huguenots (French Protestants), Presbyterians, Anglicans, Lutherans, Jews, and Catholics. The Dutch also settled northern New Jersey, but Quakers were present as well, and Scots-Irish brought Presbyterianism to the colony. The region that is now Delaware was founded by the Swedes, so Swedish Lutherans established a presence there, however brief. William Penn's "Holy Experiment" made Pennsylvania another haven for religious diversity, especially for Quakers and for German groups like the Dunkers, Mennonites, and Schwenckfelders. Maryland was founded by English

Catholics, although Puritans took over, and by the time of the Glorious Revolution the Church of England was established. Virginia was Anglican, as were colonies to the South, although other groups were present also, including Moravians, mixed with a lot of folk religious practices.

The Atlantic seaboard, in short, was a laboratory of religious diversity, so much so that when the founders contemplated the configuration of church and state for the new nation, one of their quandaries would be which religion to designate as the established church. If they chose Baptists, for example, New England would surely object. If the Church of England were to be the state religion, Baptists, Quakers, Lutherans, and others would protest. And if Thomas Jefferson's preferred religion, Unitarianism, were designated the religion of the new nation, almost everyone would rebel against that idea.

The founders in their wisdom decided against any established religion, including a generic designation of Christianity, as Patrick Henry had proposed in Virginia. James Madison led the charge against Henry's proposal, and its defeat provided a template for the nation itself, thereby securing the precious right of religious liberty. As Madison observed, "This freedom arises from that multiplicity of sects, which pervades America, and which is the best and only security for religious liberty in any society. For where there is such a variety of sects, there cannot be a majority of any one sect to oppress and persecute the rest."[3]

And the effects of this novel formulation, the separation of church and state, were soon apparent. When Alexis de Tocqueville toured the new nation in the early 1830s, he spoke with religious leaders, both clergy and lay, and learned that "to a man, they assigned primary credit for the peaceful ascendancy of religion in their country to the complete separation of church and state."[4]

Even though varieties of Christianity competed with one another—Presbyterians *versus* Methodists *versus* Catholics *versus* Baptists—the popularity of Christianity writ large went virtually unchallenged until the waning decades of the twentieth century. And the misguided response on the part of some Christian leaders in the face of religious diversity has been to change the rules in their favor—installing religious displays or the Ten Commandments on public property, for instance, or providing taxpayer money to religious schools or designating the United States as a "Christian nation."

Rather than competing in the marketplace of religion in America, many Christians, especially leaders, sought to skew the rules in their favor. But that is ultimately a losing proposition because it braids faith with the state, and that is a very dangerous proposition. The person who saw this first and most clearly was Roger Williams, a former Puritan and progenitor of the Baptist tradition in America. Williams, a graduate of Cambridge University, arrived in Boston in 1631 and settled in Salem by 1634. Very quickly, however, Williams ran afoul of the Puritan authorities in Massachusetts because he protested the close association between church and state, religion and politics, in the colony.

Williams was haled into court and convicted of "diverse, new, and dangerous opinions." He was banished from Massachusetts and headed south toward Narragansett Bay, purchased land from the Narragansett Indian Tribe, and founded Providence because of his "sense of God's merciful providence unto me in my distress." From the beginning, Williams decided that the new settlement "might be a shelter for persons distressed for conscience."[5]

Williams's restless intellect led him in the direction of Baptist ideas, which centered around adult (or believer's) baptism and liberty of conscience, or "soul liberty." At Providence in March 1639, Ezekiel Holliman baptized Williams by full immersion at the mouth of the Mooshashuck River; Williams in turn baptized Holliman and ten others, thereby founding the Baptist tradition in North America.

While visiting England to secure a charter for the colony of Rhode Island, Williams produced his most important treatise, called *The Bloudy Tenent of Persecution for the Cause of Conscience*, his reflections on the proper relationship between church and state. "When they have opened a gap in the hedge or wall of separation between the garden of the church and the wilderness of the world," Williams wrote, "God hath ever broke down the wall itself, removed the candlestick, and made His garden a wilderness, as at this day." Williams sought to protect religion from the depredations of the state, and he saw strict separation as the way to accomplish this. If God, Williams believed, "will ever please to restore His garden and paradise again, it must of necessity be walled in peculiarly unto Himself from the world; and that all that shall be saved out of the world are to be transplanted out of the wilderness of the world, and added unto His church or garden."[6]

In this memorable metaphor, Williams wanted to segregate the "garden of the church" from the "wilderness of the world" by means of a "hedge or wall of separation." Those images have become so familiar that they may have lost some of their meaning, and to understand the significance of that metaphor we must recall that the Puritans did not share our idyllic, post-Thoreauvian romantic notions about wilderness. For the colonists of the seventeenth century, struggling to carve a godly society out of the howling wilderness of Massachusetts, wilderness was a place of danger. It was a realm of darkness where evil lurked. So, when Williams wanted to protect the "garden" of the church from the "wilderness" of the world, he was concerned to preserve the integrity of the faith from defilement by too close an association with the state. Williams worried that the faith would be trivialized and fetishized when conflated with the state.

Sadly, that lesson has been lost on too many Christians in twenty-first-century America. The Southern Baptist Convention, once a vigilant watchman on the wall of separation between church and state, has largely abandoned that role since the conservative takeover in 1979. And perhaps the most egregious example of the abandonment of Baptist principles was Roy S. Moore, the notorious "Ten Commandments judge."

Moore, a former kickboxer, was appointed to fill a vacant circuit court judgeship in Gadsden, Alabama; he ran and won election to the bench in his own right in 1992. Moore opened his court sessions with prayer and hung a hand-carved wooden plaque depicting the Ten Commandments in his courtroom, an action that clearly represented an infringement of the establishment clause of the First Amendment. The American Civil Liberties Union filed suit in 1995 to have the plaque removed. The people of Alabama, however, rather than censure his flouting of the Constitution, rewarded Moore by electing him chief justice of the Alabama Supreme Court in 2000; Moore, running as a Republican, had campaigned for office as the "Ten Commandments Judge."

Shortly after his election, he commissioned a local gravestone company to produce a monument emblazoned with the Decalogue. Late in the evening of July 31, 2001, Moore and a work crew, laboring through the night, installed the two-and-one-half-ton granite monument, which would come to be known as "Roy's Rock," in the lobby of the Alabama Judicial Building in Montgomery. Moore, who claims to be a Baptist—he's not; no true Baptist would engage in such antics—steadfastly refused to allow any other religious sentiments in that space, only the Decalogue.

I was one of the expert witnesses in the so-called Ten Commandments case in Alabama. My testimony was that the

First Amendment and the separation of church and state was the best thing that ever happened to religion in the United States—and it is precisely because of the First Amendment, which allows religion to flourish. As Roger Williams warned long ago, any attempt to blur the line of separation diminishes the integrity of the faith by associating it with the state.

Myron Thompson, district judge for the Middle District of Alabama, ruled—correctly—that "Roy's Rock" violated the First Amendment and must be removed. As the workers were preparing to relocate the monument, one of the protesters screamed, "Get your hands off my God!"

I'm reasonably certain that one of the Commandments etched into the side of that monument said something about graven images. And that was precisely Roger Williams's point about protecting the faith from trivialization by too close an association with politics and the state. As another Baptist, Martin Luther King Jr., remarked, "The church must be reminded that it is not the master or the servant of the state, but rather the conscience of the state. It must be the guide and the critic of the state, and never its tool. If the church does not recapture its prophetic zeal, it will become an irrelevant social club without moral or spiritual authority."[7]

3

THE FANTASY OF CHRISTIAN NATIONALISM

My kingdom is not of this world.

—John 18:36

ONE OF ROY Moore's specious claims was that the founders intended to protect the "free exercise" of only Christianity because, he said, the founders did not know of any other religion. That statement is false, of course; the founders were well aware of other religions, including Islam. But Moore's argument has fed into the misguided frenzy to anoint the United States as a "Christian nation."

Let's cut to the chase: The United States can be deemed a "Christian nation" in only one sense, which is that a majority of Americans identify as Christian, not that the founders intended to construct a government on Christian principles. Their intention, in fact, was precisely the opposite so that new nation would not be burdened or impeded by religious factionalism or the interlocking authority of religious institutions.

Those who argue that the United States is, and always has been, a Christian nation base much of their reasoning upon the religious convictions of individual founders. First, in order to examine that claim we need to determine a standard for who is and who is not a Christian. The diversity within Christianity being what it is, I suppose we could come up with several definitions, but I can think of nothing more appropriate or universal than the Nicene Creed, adopted by a gathering of church leaders at Nicaea in 325 CE and further refined at the Council of Constantinople in 381:

> *We believe in one God, the Father, the Almighty, maker of heaven and earth, of all that is, seen and unseen.*
>
> *We believe in one Lord, Jesus Christ, the only Son of God, eternally begotten of the Father, God from God, Light from Light, true God from true God, begotten, not made, of one Being with the Father. Through him all things were made. For us and for our salvation he came down from heaven: by the power of the Holy Spirit he became incarnate from the Virgin Mary, and was made man. For our sake he was crucified under Pontius Pilate; he suffered death and was buried. On the third day he rose again in accordance with the Scriptures; he ascended into heaven and is seated at the right hand of the Father. He will come again in glory to judge the living and the dead, and his kingdom will have no end.*

> *We believe in the Holy Spirit, the Lord, the giver of life, who proceeds from the Father and the Son. With the Father and the Son he is worshiped and glorified. He has spoken through the Prophets.*
>
> *We believe in one holy catholic and apostolic Church. We acknowledge one baptism for the forgiveness of sins. We look for the resurrection of the dead, and the life of the world to come.* Amen.

This statement of faith—the wording of the Apostles' Creed varies slightly—has served as the touchstone of the Christian orthodoxy since the fourth century. How do the founders measure up to that standard?

George Washington came from a tobacco-growing family. He served as a commander in the Seven Years' (French and Indian) War and as general of the Continental Army during the Revolutionary War. Washington presided over the Continental Congress and served as the new nation's first president, from 1789 to 1797.

Washington was baptized into the Church of England, but never confirmed. He was a member of the vestry in his local parish, but rarely or never took Holy Communion. In 1752 he was initiated into the Masons, and many historians consider him a deist—someone who believes in a divine Creator, but a Creator who remains indifferent to his creation. In a 1776 letter to William Gordon, Washington wrote: "No Man has a more perfect Reliance on the alwise, and powerful dispensations of the Supreme Being than I have nor thinks his aid more necessary." For a man of his time, he harbored remarkably inclusive, or "catholic," views of other religions; in 1784, for example, Washington directed his surrogate at Mount Vernon to hire "good workmen, they may be from Asia, Africa or Europe; they may be Mahometans [Muslims], Jews, Christians of any sect, or they may be Atheists." Like other founders, especially Thomas Jefferson, Washington disliked religious factionalism. "Of all the animosities which have existed among mankind, those which are caused by difference of sentiments in religion appear to be the most inveterate and distressing, and ought most to be deprecated," Washington wrote in 1792. "I was in hopes that the enlightened and liberal policy, which has marked the present age, would at least have reconciled Christians of every denomination so far that we should never again see the religious disputes carried to such a pitch as to endanger the peace of society."[1]

John Witherspoon, born in Scotland, migrated to America in 1768 to become president of the College of New Jersey. A Presbyterian minister, he was a signer of the Declaration of Independence and a member of the Continental Congress. In 1789 he presided over the first general assembly of the Presbyterian Church.

A product of the Reformed tradition (followers of sixteenth-century theologian John Calvin), Witherspoon believed in human depravity, that all people inherit the sin of Adam. "Nothing can be more absolutely necessary to true religion than a clear and full conviction of the sinfulness of our nature and state," he wrote in 1776. "Without this there can be neither repentance in the sinner nor humility in the believer." Witherspoon was concerned that the new government clamp down on profanity and immorality; it should support "true and undefiled religion." He also discerned the connection between religion and civil liberty. "God grant that in America true religion and civil liberty may be inseparable, and that the unjust attempts to destroy the one may in the issue tend to the support and establishment of both," he wrote in 1776. Witherspoon's Thanksgiving Day proclamation in 1782 lauded "the practice of true and undefiled religion, which is the great foundation of public prosperity and national happiness."[2]

John Adams considered entering the ministry before opting to study law. Educated at Harvard, he served in the Continental Congress, as ambassador to Britain, and as Washington's vice president before his election as president in 1796. He served a single term, losing the 1800 election to Thomas Jefferson.

Though reared a Congregationalist, Adams became a Unitarian. He did not believe in the Trinity, the Christian doctrine, defined in the Nicene Creed, that God exists in three persons: Father, Son, and Holy Spirit. "My religion you know is not exactly conformable to that of the greatest part of the Christian World," Adams acknowledged in a letter to his wife, Abigail, in 1799. "It excludes superstition. But with all the superstition that attends it, I think the Christian the best that is or has been." Adams understood the value of religion. "I have attended public worship in all countries and with all sects and believe them all much better than no religion," he wrote to Benjamin Rush, "though I have not thought myself obliged to believe all I heard." The second president's most candid remarks about faith appeared in a letter to his son, John Quincy Adams, in 1816. "An incarnate God ! ! ! An eternal, self-existent, omnipresent omniscient Author of this stupendous Universe, suffering on a Cross! ! ! My Soul starts with horror, at the Idea, and it has stupified the Christian World. It has been the Source of almost all the Corruptions of Christianity."[3]

Benjamin Franklin, born in Boston and reared a Calvinist, moved to Philadelphia in 1723. He joined the Masons in 1730, was a member of the Continental Congress, and served as minister to France in 1799.

Franklin counted George Whitefield, one of the catalysts of the Great Awakening, among his friends; Franklin was Whitefield's publisher, and he contributed financially to Whitefield's efforts. Franklin understood the utility of religion, which he believed should issue in morality. As early as 1735, he wrote: "No point of Faith is so plain, as that *Morality* is our Duty; for all Sides agree in that. A virtuous Heretick shall be saved before a wicked Christian." Franklin developed this notion in a letter to Whitefield in 1753: "The faith you mention has doubtless its use in the world. I do not desire to see it diminished, nor would I desire to lessen it in any way; but I wish it were more productive of good works than I have generally seen it. I mean real good works, works of kindness, charity, mercy, and public spirit, not holy-day keeping, sermon-hearing, and reading, performing church ceremonies, or making long prayers, filled with flatteries and compliments, despised even by wise men, and much less capable of pleasing the Deity."[4]

Franklin's letter to Ezra Stiles, dated March 9, 1790, provides the most comprehensive peek into his views about the divinity of Jesus. "As to Jesus of Nazareth, my opinion of whom you particularly desire, I think his system of morals and his religion, as he left them to us, the best the world ever saw or is likely to see," Franklin wrote, "but I apprehend it has received various corrupting changes, and I have, with most of the present dissenters in England, some doubts as to his divinity; though it is a question I do not dogmatize upon, having never studied it, and think it needless to busy myself with it now, when I expect soon an opportunity of knowing the truth with less trouble. I see no harm, however, in its being believed, if that belief has the good consequences, as probably it has, of making his doctrines more respected and more observed."[5]

Thomas Jefferson graduated from the College of William and Mary. He served in Virginia's House of Burgesses and the Continental Congress. He was minister to France, secretary of state, vice president under John Adams, and president for two terms, beginning in 1801.

Jefferson, a creature of the Enlightenment, was a deist who thought the Church of England was too privileged. His most famous religious venture was to excise any mention of miracles or Jesus's divinity from the Gospels; he published what remained as *The Life and Morals of Jesus of Nazareth Extracted Textually from the Gospels*, better known simply as the Jefferson Bible. He characterized his depiction of Jesus as "a paradigm of his doctrines, made by cutting the texts out of the book, and arranging them on the pages of a blank book, in a certain order of time or subject. A more beautiful or precious morsel of ethics I have never seen."[6]

In an 1803 letter to Benjamin Rush, Jefferson wrote: "To the corruptions of Christianity I am indeed opposed; but not to the genuine precepts of Jesus himself. I am a Christian, in the only sense he wished any one to be; sincerely attached to his doctrines, in preference to all others; ascribing to himself every *human* excellence; & believing he never claimed any other." Some years later, he wrote: "I am a *real Christian*, that is to say a disciple of the doctrines of Jesus." As with Franklin, Jefferson believed that good works lay at the center of any religion worthy of the name. "My fundamental principle would be the reverse of Calvin's," Jefferson wrote to Thomas B. Parker in 1819, "that we are to be saved by our good works which are within our power, and not by our faith which is not within our power." Finally, Jefferson predicted that his fellow Americans would come to reject religious superstition generally and especially the notion of Jesus's divinity. "I trust that there is not a young man now living in the US who will not die an Unitarian," Jefferson wrote just four years before his death.[7]

James Madison, sometimes called the father of the Constitution, was a member of Congress, drafted the Bill of Rights, and served as secretary of state. He was elected to the presidency in 1808 and reelected four years later. Like Washington, Madison was reared an Anglican, but never confirmed. He attended the College of New Jersey and, like Adams, briefly considered the ministry. He studied law and politics instead.

Madison's religious views are somewhat enigmatic, but he was a fierce opponent of religious establishments. "Ecclesiastical establishments tend to great ignorance and corruption," he wrote in 1774, before the Declaration of Independence, "all of which facilitate the execution of mischievous projects." It was Madison's *Memorial and Remonstrance* that turned the tide against Patrick Henry's attempt to establish Christianity in Virginia, even though Madison characterized Christianity as the "best & purest religion." Like other founders, Madison considered religion conducive to "the moral order of the world and to the happiness of man."[8]

The scorecard? Of all the founders surveyed here, only John Witherspoon fits comfortably within the Christian tradition as defined by the Nicene Creed—and even he, as a Presbyterian, might quibble with the phrase about "one holy catholic and apostolic Church." Washington and Madison are possibilities, although their churchgoing habits were unconventional. John Adams, a Unitarian, could not affirm the divinity of Jesus, nor did Franklin or Jefferson.

To put the matter in other terms, with the possible exception of Witherspoon, none of the founders would qualify for membership in the churches attended by those affiliated with Christian nationalist movement.

If the assertion of the United States as a Christian nation rests on the piety and the orthodoxy of the individual founders, that argument teeters on a somewhat less than solid foundation. That hasn't stopped many Christian leaders from pressing the case, sometimes, as with David Barton, by means of manufactured quotations or quotes wrenched out of context, malpractice so egregious that his very conservative publisher, Thomas Nelson, withdrew his book from circulation.

Even if we grant the piety of the founders—a huge concession!—the Christian nationalists still must maneuver around the First Amendment ("Congress shall make no law respecting an establishment of religion") and the Treaty of Tripoli, which represents an even higher hurdle.

In 1796, the final full year of George Washington's presidency, the United States negotiated the Treaty of Tripoli in an attempt to shield American merchant ships sailing along the Barbary Coast. The treaty was signed in Tripoli on November 4, 1796, and again at Algiers on January 3, 1797. Article 11 reads as follows:

*As the government of the United States of America
is not in any sense founded on the Christian
Religion,—as it has in itself no character of
enmity against the laws, religion or tranquility of
Musselmen [Muslims],—and as the said States never
have entered into any war or act of hostility against
any Mehomitan [Islamic] nation, it is declared by
the parties that no pretext arising from religious
opinions shall ever produce an interruption of the
harmony existing between the two countries.*

The Treaty of Tripoli was read aloud in the United States Senate and copies provided for every senator. John Adams, the president, added his endorsement, requiring "all other citizens or inhabitants thereof, faithfully to observe and fulfill the said Treaty and every clause and article thereof." The Senate ratified the Treaty of Tripoli unanimously, without debate, on June 7, 1797.[9]

The language of Article 11 is manifestly clear—"the government of the United States of America is not in any sense founded on the Christian Religion"—so anyone arguing that the United States *is* a Christian nation would need to explain away both Article 11 of the Treaty of Tripoli and the Senate's unanimous ratification of the treaty. Clearly, those who constituted the government in the early years of the new nation—the executive and legislative branches—had no quarrel with the statement that the United States was not founded on Christianity.

The rebuttals of Christian nationalists are tortured, but they appear to rely on quoting the entirety of Article 11 (reproduced above *in its entirety*), not merely the opening phrase: "As the government of the United States of America is not in any sense founded on the Christian Religion. . . ." Fair enough. Context is always important. It's not clear to me, however, how the full article in any way changes the plain meaning of the phrase. The treaty makes the case that the United States has no "enmity" against Islam or Muslims. The treaty does not assert that the United States is a Christian nation; it states the opposite: "the government of the United States of America is not in any sense founded on the Christian Religion."

The arguments for Christian nationalism falter on several fronts: a plain reading of the Treaty of Tripoli and the First Amendment itself, as well as the ideology and religious convictions of the founders.

4

RECLAIMING THE FAITH

And forgive us our debts, as we also have forgiven our debtors.

—Matthew 6:12

IF CHRISTIANS SERIOUSLY seek a revitalization of their faith in America, it will come not by means of legal or judicial coercion or through fraudulent claims about the United States as a Christian nation. It will happen instead when Christians themselves acknowledge the mistakes of the past and reaffiliate with the best of their tradition.

Please understand that I am not suggesting that contemporary Christians must shoulder responsibility for the actions of believers in the past—although the notion of reparations should be part of the conversation. Individuals bear responsibility for their own actions. At the same time, we must acknowledge that those who claimed the banner of Christianity in the past have sometimes behaved in less than edifying ways, and we should also reckon with the fact that we, especially white Christians, have benefited systemically, economically, and politically from the prejudices and the oppressions perpetrated in decades and centuries past.

Make no mistake, Christians have done much good in the world in the name of their faith: alleviating poverty and disease, mediating conflict, promoting beauty through aesthetics. Missionaries have provided health care, literacy, housing, and sustainable agricultural practices to Third World peoples. The Anglican choral tradition, with its soaring descants, to take one example, represents one of the aesthetic highlights of the Christian tradition. Christianity can also claim to have inspired beautiful architecture and worthy literature, and people who have taken the words of Jesus seriously have worked diligently to make the world a better place.

But honesty and integrity require that we acknowledge an underside as well. The Crusades typically fall into this category, a time when, from the eleventh through the thirteenth centuries, bands of Christian warriors sought to reclaim the sacred sites of the Holy Land from Muslims, exacting a fearsome toll of casualties. The Inquisition intersected with the Crusades, beginning in the twelfth century, directed first against the Cathars in southern France and the Waldensians in Germany and northern Italy. The Spanish Inquisition was especially brutal, with over thirty-two thousand executions. The Inquisition targeted Muslims and *conversos*, Jews suspected of converting to Christianity under false pretenses, as well as figures like Joan of Arc, who was burned at the stake in 1431. The Inquisition also expanded to the New World in

1570, where Protestants were tortured and sometimes burned alive.

At times, Christians persecuted other Christians. During the era of the Protestant Reformation, for example, both Protestants and Catholics targeted the Anabaptists, who believe in adult (believers') baptism. Not infrequently the penalty for being an Anabaptist was a third baptism, the first being baptism by sprinkling as an infant (the traditional Roman Catholic and Protestant practice), the second being baptism by full immersion as an adult believer, and the third by drowning for flouting the law. The Wars of Religion in France, including the St. Bartholomew's Day Massacre in 1572, exacted a fearsome toll on both sides of the Protestant–Catholic divide.

In the American context, we must reckon with Christian complicity in the abuse, removal, and murder of Native peoples. Bartolomé de las Casas's *A Short Account of the Destruction of the Indies*, published in 1552, chronicles in chilling detail the atrocities of Spanish conquistadors in seeking to subdue and to Christianize the indigenous peoples of the Americas. The Spanish colonizing strategy of *encomienda*, which granted conquerors the right to forced labor of conquered non-Christian people, was slavery in all but name.

English settlers were no better. New England Puritans, under the guidance of John Eliot and Daniel Gookin, segregated American Indian converts into "praying towns," although the converts were largely abandoned during King Phillip's War between Puritans and American Indians, the bloodiest war per capita in American history. The Dutch Reformed in New Netherland and the Quakers of Pennsylvania treated Native Americans marginally better, but a group of Pennsylvania militiamen killed ninety-six Christianized Delaware Indians in what became known as the Gnadenhutten Massacre of 1782.

The overall narrative of Christian–Indian relations is a sorry one, a story of domination, cultural imperialism, sadistic savagery, and broken promises. Those characteristics continued into the nineteenth century and beyond. The doctrine of Manifest Destiny, the notion that the United States possessed a divine mandate to expand the breadth of the continent to the Pacific Ocean and push aside Native Americans, led to such displacements as the Black Hawk War of 1832 and the Trail of Tears. As an army general, Andrew Jackson had led brutal campaigns against the Seminoles in Florida and the Creeks in Alabama and Georgia; as president, he signed the Indian Removal Act of 1830, which eventually forced various tribes in the Southeast to relocate to present-day Oklahoma. As many as fifteen thousand may have perished on the Trail of Tears. John Chivington, a former Methodist minister and missionary to the Wyandot Nation in Kansas, led the Sand Creek Massacre against Cheyennes and Arapahoes on November 29, 1864. "I have come to kill Indians," Chivington declared, "and believe it is right and honorable to use any means under God's heavens to kill Indians."[1]

Christians played a more direct role in the American Indian boarding schools of the nineteenth century. Congress passed the Indian Civilization Act Fund in 1819, which appropriated funds for missionaries and church leaders to cooperate with the federal government to provide education aimed at replacing tribal practices with Christianity. The Bureau of Indian Affairs established the first boarding school on the Yakima Indian Reservation in 1860, using education as a tool to assimilate and "civilize" Native children into the "American way of life." The Peace Policy of 1869, under Ulysses S. Grant, accelerated the proliferation of boarding schools, the most famous of which, the Carlisle Indian Industrial School, was founded in 1879 by Richard Henry Pratt, a former Union officer in the Civil War. Pratt's motto was "Kill the Indian, Save the Man," a strategy he pursued by compelling students, many of them forcibly removed from their families and communities, to cut their hair, wear European clothing, and forsake Native customs. Students were forbidden to speak their Native languages, and anyone who resisted these measures met with harsh discipline, including solitary confinement.

Pratt's tactics were widely adopted by other schools, many of them operated by Christian denominations. By 1926, nearly 83 percent of Native school-age children were attending boarding schools. Recent revelations about the abuses of such schools, in both the United States and Canada, have touched off inquiries into both the disappearance of Native students and the cultural genocide perpetrated at these institutions.[2]

Historians often refer to slavery and racism as America's "original sin." The forcible removal of Africans across the Atlantic to lives of involuntary servitude surely qualifies as one of the most egregious violations of human dignity in all of history. Sadly, Christians were complicit in this outrage, and Christian theologians even offered theological defenses of slavery, most often centered around the so-called curse of Ham in the book of Genesis, St. Paul's letter to Philemon asking that he accept a returning slave without recrimination, and Paul's admonition in Colossians and Ephesians for slaves to obey their earthly masters. These same theologians pay correspondingly little attention to the story of Exodus or to Paul's declaration in Galatians that in Christ there is no distinction between Jew or Gentile, slave or free, male or female.[3]

James Henley Thornwell, a slaveholder, a Presbyterian, and professor at Columbia Theological Seminary, offered his defense of slavery, arguing that it has "the sanction of the oracles of God." Moreover, it was ubiquitous. "Slavery exists, of course, in every nation in which it is not prohibited," he wrote in 1860. "It arose, in the progress of human events, from the operation of moral causes; it has been grounded by philosophers in moral maxims; it has always been held to be moral by the vast majority of the race. No age has been without it." Slavery, moreover, produced the greater good of conversion to Christianity, Thornwell asserted: ". . . we cannot but accept it as a gracious providence that they have been brought in such numbers to our shores and redeemed from the bondage of barbarism and sin. Slavery to them has certainly been over-ruled for the greatest good. It has been a link in the wondrous chain of providence, through which many sons and daughters have been made heirs of the heavenly inheritance."[4]

One of the most famous defenders of slavery was Robert Louis Dabney, a Presbyterian pastor and theology professor at Union Theological Seminary, in Richmond, Virginia, and a chaplain in the Confederate army. "Christ's giving the law of love cannot be inconsistent with his authorizing slaveholding," Dabney wrote, "because Moses gave the same law of love, and yet indisputably authorized slaveholding." Slavery, Dabney argued, improved the morals of Africans, who were depraved and pagan before being exposed to Christianity. "Now cannot common sense see the moral advantage to such a people, of subjection to the will of a race elevated above them, in morals and intelligence, to an almost measureless degree?" Servitude, in fact, should be credited with advancing the Christian faith. "This much-abused system has accomplished for the Africans, amidst universal opposition and obloquy," Dabney argued, "more than all of the rest of the Christian world altogether has accomplished for the rest of the heathen."[5]

Other theologians echoed these views. Basil Manly Sr., Baptist minister and longtime president of the University of Alabama, wrote the "Alabama Resolutions" in defense of slavery. Manly was one of the leaders of the Baptist seces-sion in 1845 to form the Southern Baptist Convention, and he served as official chaplain to the Confederacy. Thornton

Stringfellow, a Baptist preacher in Virginia and son of a slave-holder, wrote a book, *A Brief Examination of Scripture Testimony on the Institution of Slavery*, published in 1850, arguing that Jesus did not prohibit slavery and that nothing in his teachings mandated the elimination of slavery.

Patrick Lynch, Roman Catholic bishop of Charleston, South Carolina, acquired his first slaves in 1857 and then inherited several plantations and a large number of slaves from the estate of a parishioner in 1861. He regarded the institution of slavery as benign, and he argued that "free negroes are far more immoral than the slaves." Lynch, however, refused to sell slaves if doing so would break up families. The founders of the University of the South in 1857, an Episcopal school, were ardent apologists for slavery. Nor were Christian defenses of slavery confined to the South. In 1864, for example, John Henry Hopkins, Episcopal bishop in Vermont, published a theological defense of slavery.[6]

The Emancipation Proclamation and the conclusion of the Civil War may have brought a legal end to slavery, but the effects of racial prejudice continue to the present, illustrated once again by the murders of George Floyd, Breonna Taylor, and Ahmaud Arbery, among many others. The formation of the Ku Klux Klan in 1865, cloaked in "Christian" theology, the proliferation of Black codes, extra-legal lynchings, and Jim Crow laws perpetrated the fiction that people of color were somehow inferior. Protestant ministers were also involved in the recrudescence of the Klan in the early decades of the twentieth century. Thomas Dixon Jr., a Baptist minister, published *The Clansman: A Historical Romance of the Ku Klux Klan* in 1905, which celebrated white supremacy and inspired D. W. Griffith's racist classic film, *Birth of a Nation*, which was released in 1915. Dixon (whose brother, A. C. Dixon, was one of the editors of *The Fundamentals*) also inspired a Methodist preacher, William Joseph Simmons, to revive the Klan with a Thanksgiving night 1915 cross-burning on Stone Mountain. Simmons anointed himself imperial wizard of the revived organization, dedicated to "the perpetual preservation of the fundamental principles, ideals and institutions of the pure Anglo-Saxon civilization and all the fruits thereof."[7]

Sadly, white supremacy mixed with putative Christianity has persisted throughout the twentieth and into the twenty-first century. An estimated forty thousand Protestant ministers, including Alma Bridwell White, joined the second iteration of the Ku Klux Klan during its heyday in the early 1920s. Evangelist Robert "Fighting Bob" Shuler of Los Angeles characterized Klan rhetoric "as sweet music as my ears have ever heard," and one of the Klan's largest donations was to whites-only Bob Jones College (now University), which was founded on the conviction that God intended the races to be separate. Bob Jones Sr. supported Klansman Bibb Graves's campaign for governor of Alabama, and Graves reciprocated by delivering the keynote address at the school's groundbreaking in 1926. Klansmen Sam Bowers Jr. and Edgar Ray "Preacher" Killen claimed to be doing God's work in unleashing unspeakable violence, including murder, against African Americans, all because of their conviction that Blacks were inferior.[8]

Ethnic essentialism persists in the twenty-first century, whether directed against Native Americans, Blacks, Hispanics, or immigrants in general. "There's ethnic specialization in crime," Peter Brimelow, president of an anti-immigrant organization and professed Christian, declared in 2017. "And Hispanics do specialize in rape, particularly of children. They're very prone to it, compared to other groups."[9]

Without question, Christians have worked to make the world a better place. But any sober assessment of the influence of Christianity in America must also take into account some of the less savory chapters in our history. The purpose is not to impute guilt to individuals long removed from earlier abuses, but to acknowledge that exploitations and atrocities have been perpetrated by others in the name of the Christian faith—and to recognize that the sins of earlier generations have helped to create a system of inequality in which some benefit to the detriment of others.

5

BACK TO THE BIBLE

Truly I tell you, whatever you did for one of the least of these brothers and sisters of mine, you did for me.

—Matthew 25:40

FOR CHRISTIANS THROUGH the centuries, the Bible—the sixty-six books of the Hebrew Bible and the New Testament—has provided a lodestar for Christian faith and practice, however imperfectly understood or appropriated. Christians regard Holy Scripture as God's revelation to humanity; it provides the basis of authority for both Catholics and Protestants, although Martin Luther's assertion of *sola scriptura*—the Bible alone—as the source of authority removed the church, the Roman Catholic Church, as the authoritative interpreter of scripture and vested that function in individuals, those Luther called the priesthood of believers.

To underscore that point, many Protestants, evangelicals in particular, refer to the Bible as the *Word of God*, whereas other believers might argue, on the basis of the first chapter of John's Gospel, that *Jesus* is the Word of God: "In the beginning was the Word, and the Word was with God, and the

Word was God. He was with God in the beginning." If we take seriously that *Jesus* is the Word of God, therefore, then to understand the Almighty we must look first to the life and teachings of Jesus. In either case, whether you believe that the Bible is the Word of God or Jesus is the Word of God—or both—all Christians agree that the Bible is indispensable to understanding their faith.[1]

How curious, then, that so many Christians seem to have neglected the Bible and what it has to say about issues that we as a society face in the twenty-first century. If we Christians entertain any hopes of reviving the faith and making Christianity relevant once again, we must find a way to reconnect with the Scriptures.

The writings of ancient Israel, collected in the Hebrew Bible, are rich and varied. The Hebrew Bible contains the accounts of creation (Genesis) as well as the sufferings of Job, generally considered the oldest of all the writings. It includes poetry and lamentations, love songs and codes of conduct, a history of the wanderings of the Israelites and the warnings of the prophets.

Let's begin at the beginning. The creation stories in the opening chapters of Genesis have long attracted attention, though arguably for the wrong reasons. Those who insist on interpreting the Bible literally are compelled to explain why the first creation narrative differs from the second. I recall enduring a very long lecture at my evangelical seminary from an Old Testament professor who contended that no, despite all appearances to the contrary, it was a single narrative, not two. These same literalists—although most literalists, in my experience, engage in *selective* literalism—argue that the world came into existence in seven twenty-four-hour days, as recorded in the first creation story: God created the heavens and the earth on day one, and so on.

The publication of Charles Darwin's *Origin of Species* in 1859 dealt a blow to traditional, literal interpretations of Genesis, and it's not difficult to see why. While many believers saw no contradiction between Darwin's theory of evolution and the first Genesis account—the Almighty could work through the evolutionary process, or "days" could be interpreted as longer periods of time—other believers regarded Darwin as a threat to the integrity of the Bible and doubled down on the seven days of creation. That position, in turn, has fueled the culture wars, with various attempts to mandate the teaching of some form of "creationism" in public schools.

These culture wars have played out in communities, school boards, and the courts for a century now. The infamous Scopes Trial in the summer of 1925 pitted Clarence Darrow against William Jennings Bryan in Dayton, Tennessee, over the teaching of evolution in public schools. Although the creationists ostensibly won the case—John T. Scopes was convicted of violating the state's Butler Act and fined $100—evangelicals lost decisively in the larger courtroom of public opinion. Creationists, however, were undeterred, and as the courts have consistently turned back the teaching of creationism as a species of religion—which, of course, it is—creationists have shifted their ground. When "creationism" was outlawed, they proposed "scientific creationism," then "intelligent design," thereby providing the most irrefutable proof of "evolution" I've ever witnessed![2]

In my view, however, the debate over creation overlooks the larger point of Genesis; it's a classic case of missing the forest for the trees. The creation accounts in Genesis make no claim to be history, much less science. These creation accounts are far too important to be reduced to science or history. They are stories meant to tell us something crucial about God, humanity, and the created order. To reduce these stories to literalism diminishes them.

So, what might it mean if we approach the Genesis accounts of creation seriously rather than literally? First, we gain a fuller appreciation of the Almighty as creator, and we also learn that humanity stands at the pinnacle of creation. But we also come away with greater respect for the created order as God's handiwork, whether it came about *ex nihilo* (out of nothing) or by means of evolutionary process, or some combination of the two. But the even larger picture is that those of us who claim allegiance to the Almighty bear some responsibility to care for the created order, God's handiwork. This, in turn, has implications for environmental protection, for how we sustain ourselves and our families, for how we treat other living beings, and for the battle against the ravages of climate change.

Many Christians, especially in recent years, have gravitated to the book of Leviticus to condemn same-sex relationships. Surely, a case can be made; two texts in particular appear to be unequivocal. But we run once again into the ruse of selective literalism. The purity codes of Leviticus mandate the death penalty for adultery, for instance, and they prohibit tattoos, the consumption of pork and shellfish, planting two kinds of seed in the same field, and the wearing of clothing made of different fabrics. Someone who wears a combination cotton-polyester shirt, for example, violates Levitical laws. Two entire chapters in Leviticus address the matter of infectious skin diseases, which are to be reported to the priest, whereas only two verses pertain to same-sex relationships.[3]

The book of Leviticus also demands that portions of the harvest be left for the poor and that nothing be done to pervert justice. "The foreigner residing among you must be treated as your native-born," according to Leviticus. "Love them as yourself, for you were foreigners in Egypt." And to underscore the point, the passage continues, "I am the Lord your God." Issues of borders and national sovereignty are complex, but surely this passage, with its injunction to love foreigners, bears some relevance to the issue of refugees and immigration.[4]

The Hebrew Bible has a great deal to say about justice and inequality. In Exodus, we read, "Do not deny justice to your poor people in their lawsuits," and Deuteronomy says, "Cursed is anyone who withholds justice from the foreigner, the fatherless or the widow." Proverbs tells us, "The righteous care about justice for the poor, but the wicked have no such concern," and, "When justice is done, it brings joy to the righteous but terror to evildoers."[5]

The Hebrew prophets were especially attuned to matters of justice, often linking justice to the treatment of the poor. "Learn to do right; seek justice," Isaiah says. "Defend the oppressed. Take up the cause of the fatherless; plead the case of the widow." Jeremiah laments that the people of Jerusalem no longer seek justice; in addition, "They do not promote the case of the fatherless; they do not defend the just cause of the poor." Ezekiel complains, "The people of the land practice extortion and commit robbery; they oppress the poor and needy and mistreat the foreigner, denying them justice." Amos instructs the people of Israel to hate evil, love good, and "maintain justice," and Zechariah delivers this message from the Lord: "Administer true justice; show mercy and compassion to one another."[6]

These admonitions are representative, not exhaustive; I could have quoted dozens of others—far, far more than any declarations about same-sex relations, by the way. The sheer volume of biblical evidence suggests that issues of justice are very important to the Almighty.

It should not be surprising that Jesus, a first-century Jew, repeated many of the themes from the Hebrew Bible. In the temple, Jesus quoted Isaiah, declaring that he had been anointed "to proclaim good news to the poor. He has sent me to proclaim freedom for the prisoners and recovery of sight for the blind, to set the oppressed free, to proclaim the year of the Lord's favor." Jesus repeatedly criticized the Jewish leaders of his day for failing to pursue justice, warning them that, in their zealous defense of the law, they had "neglected the more important matters of the law—justice, mercy and faithfulness."[7]

Jesus even suggests that the criteria for entering the kingdom of heaven are focused on how we treat those less fortunate. On the day of judgment, he says, God will allocate rewards dependent on our actions toward those Jesus called "the least of these," and the Almighty takes this personally: "For I was hungry and you gave me something to eat, I was thirsty and you gave me something to drink, I was a stranger and you invited me in, I needed clothes and you clothed me, I was sick and you looked after me, I was in prison and you came to visit me."[8]

Once again, the words of Jesus should have some bearing on contemporary issues such as immigration, homelessness, health care, and prison reform.

We can also learn something from the way Jesus treated others, especially women and those in need of healing. Although it is certainly true that, in the context of a patriarchal society, Jesus chose men as his disciples, we have no evidence from the Gospels that he regarded women as less than equal. On matters of sexual identity and practice, Jesus said nothing at all.[9]

I've long argued that you could create a pretty reliable taxonomy of the Christian faith by charting which groups gravitate to which portions of the Bible. Roman Catholics and many mainline Protestants, for example, tend to focus on the Gospels, which contain a record of the life and teachings of Jesus. Evangelicals, on the other hand, drift toward the New Testament epistles, especially the writings of St. Paul, as well as to the ethical tables contained in the first five books of the Hebrew Bible, also known as the Torah or Pentateuch. Paul was a crucial figure in the history of Christianity; you can plausibly argue that the Christian faith might not have survived the first century were it not for Paul, who systematized the faith and sought to rein in some of the unruly elements in the various churches. Paul was also a moralist, and some Christians like his writings because they tell them how to behave.

But a full appreciation of the Bible summons us to consider also the words of the Hebrew prophets and their calls to repentance and justice, as well as the example and the teachings of Jesus. Any such understanding of the Scriptures will surely produce a more robust appropriation of the faith.

6

WORTHY EXAMPLES

Therefore, since we are surrounded by such a great cloud of witnesses, let us throw off everything that hinders and the sin that so easily entangles. And let us run with perseverance the race marked out for us. . . .

—Hebrews 12:1

IF CHRISTIANITY IS once again to become relevant to the twenty-first century, not only must believers reconnect with the Bible, they must also reaffiliate with the best of their tradition. The rollcall of faith over the centuries includes many individuals and movements worthy of emulation, as well as more than a few scoundrels. The Bible itself teaches that no one, apart from Jesus himself, perfectly embodies the faith, but we can learn from those who have sought to follow his example.

We could, of course, start with the disciples themselves and the saints, both Catholic and Orthodox, in centuries past, as well as individuals such as William Wilberforce, the member of Parliament who persuaded his colleagues in 1807 to abolish the slave trade in the British West Indies. Wilberforce and his evangelical colleagues in what became known as the Clapham

Sect also advocated for prison reform and the abolition of lotteries. A tablet on the north wall of Holy Trinity Church on Clapham Common honors those "Servants of Christ" who "laboured so abundantly for the increase of National Righteousness."[1]

Because the focus of this book is the United States, however, I will confine my examples to American society. Once again, this roster is meant to be representative, not comprehensive. Many more individuals and movements might be included here.

When we think of Christian leaders from the colonial period, the names George Whitefield, Theodorus Jacobus Frelinghuysen, Gilbert Tennent, and Jonathan Edwards come to mind, as well as various itinerant preachers. These individuals understood their task as spreading the gospel by means of proclamation and (especially in the case of Edwards) writing. They were enormously successful. Whitefield's extempory preaching became the model for evangelical oratory to the present, and Edwards has been called the greatest mind ever on the American shore.[2]

Whitefield founded and supported an orphanage in Georgia, but both he and Edwards were slaveholders, underscoring the point about the complexity of human behavior. Edwards's followers, however, including his son Jonathan Edwards Jr. and Samuel Hopkins, were dedicated opponents of slavery. The religious crusade against slavery in America was led by Quakers, and the Society of Friends, believing that the "inner light" came equally to all, were also leaders in the campaign for women's equality, especially Lucretia Mott and Susan B. Anthony. Protestants in the antebellum period supported women's rights, even voting rights, then considered a radical idea. As a minister argued in the *Oberlin Quarterly Review*, a woman should take "her rightful place *beside* (not beneath) her equal brother man"; the same writer called for the extension of suffrage to women, linking the absence of such rights to the denial of rights to African Americans. "One is forcibly reminded of the logic by which our brother is denied his rights," he wrote.[3]

Christians searching for worthy role models could do worse than Elijah H. Pilcher, a Methodist minister in Michigan. In 1841, as president of the board of trustees, he laid the cornerstone for the foundation of the first building of what would be called Albion College, known then as "The Wesleyan Seminary at Albion and Albion Female Collegiate Institute." The school admitted both sexes, but it paid particular attention to the education of women. Pilcher, like other Protestants in the nineteenth century, was a passionate advocate for public education, known then as "common schools," because they provided a way for children of those less fortunate to become upwardly mobile. "Common schools are the glory of our land," a writer declared in the *Christian Spectator*, "where even the beggar's child is taught to read, and write, and think, for himself." Pilcher served on the board of regents for the University of Michigan and vigorously opposed slavery. In 1852 he published a pamphlet entitled "The Unconstitutionality of Slavery and the Fugitive Slave Law." According to his son and biographer, Pilcher "was always on the side of humanity and freedom."[4]

By any reckoning, the most important and influential Christian in nineteenth-century America was Charles Grandison Finney, a lawyer who became a Presbyterian minister following his evangelical conversion in 1821. Finney arrived in Rochester, New York, in September 1830, and soon reports of a religious awakening in upstate New York began to circulate the nation. Finney, however, was not content with religious conversions; he believed that a regenerated life, in obedience to the teachings of Jesus, would issue in acts of benevolence toward others. "God's rule requires universal benevolence," he wrote. "I abhor a piety which has no humanity with it and in it," he added. "God loves both piety and humanity."[5]

Many Christian sentiments in the antebellum period would be considered radical by the standards of both the twentieth and twenty-first centuries, especially on the matter of free-market capitalism. Finney's understanding of the Christian faith and duty led him to a suspicion of capitalism because it was suffused with avarice and selfishness, a critique shared by many Roman Catholics. Finney allowed that, "the business aims and practices of business men are almost universally an abomination in the sight of God." What are the principles of those who engage in business? Finney asked. "Seeking their own ends; doing something not for others, but for self." Finney enumerated "another thing which is highly esteemed among men, yet is an abomination before God," namely, "selfish ambition."[6]

An evangelical farmer, writing from Vermont in 1837, offered corroboration, citing the deleterious effects of "wild speculations, arising from an undue anxiety to be hastily rich." An article in the *New-York Evangelist* similarly took a dim view of acquisitive wealth, arguing "that the believer who devotes all that is given him beyond his present necessities to the cause of Christian benevolence, trusting God for the supply of his future wants, acts more according to the mind of Christ, than he who treasures up of his abundance as a future provision for himself or family." The *Christian Chronicle* expressed similar reservations. "Riches, alas! are often amassed by the arts of oppression, extortion and deceit," the article warned. "Thus acquired, the blessing of heaven cannot rest upon them."[7]

These warnings stand in marked contrast to the so-called prosperity gospel. They also challenge the assumption, shared by many contemporary Christians, that material wealth, as Jerry Falwell once declared, is "God's way of blessing people who put him first."[8]

Although many Christians in the South defended slavery, the roster of abolitionists in the North is extensive, including such luminaries as Theodore Dwight Weld; Sarah and Angelina Grimké (refugees from Charleston, South Carolina); Josiah Bushnell Grinnell, Congregational minister and founder of Iowa

College, later renamed in his honor; and Jonathan Blanchard, Presbyterian minister and founder of Wheaton College, in Illinois. Two African Americans, Absalom Jones, an Episcopal priest, and Richard Allen, founder of the breakaway African Methodist Episcopal Church, worked tirelessly to end the scourge of slavery.

The nineteenth-century enterprise to reform society according to the norms of godliness took many forms, including public education, women's rights, peace crusades, and prison reform. We regard the temperance movement today as overweening and paternalistic, but it was at least in part a response to the rampant alcohol consumption in antebellum America and the concomitant problems of child and spousal abuse. As the nation headed into the twentieth century, liberal Christianity joined with the progressive movement to enact child labor laws, to advocate for a six-day work week, to support the rights of workers to organize, and to promote civic reform in the age of industrialization and urbanization. The religious dimension of this movement became known as the Social Gospel, with its conviction that Jesus can save not only sinful individuals, but sinful social institutions as well.

The Social Gospel fell out of favor following the Bolshevik Revolution of 1917, but it was revived in the 1940s and 1950s by Howard Thurman and a young Baptist minister named Martin Luther King Jr. The civil rights movement is populated with heroic figures who drew on their Christian faith in the struggle for equal rights: King himself, Fannie Lou Hamer, Joseph Lowrey, Hosea Williams, Fred Shuttlesworth,

Ralph David Abernathy, Andrew Young, and many others, many of them ordained ministers. John Lewis, a Baptist minister who led the march across the Edmund Pettus Bridge on Bloody Sunday, became involved in the civil rights struggle while he was a student at American Baptist Theological Seminary, in Nashville.

The rich tradition of Catholic Social Teaching extends at least as far back as the 1891 papal encyclical *Rerum Novarum* ("On the condition of labor"). As articulated and practiced by Dorothy Day, John Ryan, Thomas Merton, and others, Catholic Social Teaching prioritizes the needs of the poor and the vulnerable, emphasizes care for God's creation, the importance of community, the rights of workers, and the dignity of human life, which has often expressed itself in opposition to abortion, capital punishment, and euthanasia.

Many others could be included here. Together with her husband and other members of a Bible study group, Ida B. Wells, an African American journalist born into slavery who called attention to the epidemic of lynchings in the American South, established the Negro Fellowship League, a Black settlement house in Chicago to assist African Americans during the Great Migration to the North. Reared in New Hebron, in the Piney Woods section of central Mississippi, John M. Perkins decamped for southern California after police shot and killed his older brother, Clyde, while he stood in the alleyway queue for the "colored" entrance to Carolyn's Theater in the summer of 1946. Perkins's evangelical faith prompted him to return to

Mississippi in 1960 to promote racial healing and reconciliation. Ten years later Perkins was lured to the Rankin County jail and beaten nearly to death, but he persevered and established evangelical social-service organizations in Jackson and Mendenhall, Mississippi.[9]

The 1970s produced a number of worthy Christian examples. At the behest of Ronald J. Sider, a professor at Eastern Baptist (now Palmer) Theological Seminary and, later, author of *Rich Christians in an Age of Hunger*, forty evangelical leaders gathered at the YMCA on Wabash Street in Chicago in November 1973. Over the course of several days, they hammered out a statement, the Chicago Declaration of Evangelical Social Concern, an attempt to summon their fellow evangelicals back to the principles that had informed their movement in the nineteenth century. The declaration decried militarism and the persistence of racism in American life, as well as the scandal that people were going hungry in such an affluent society. It condemned "materialism of our culture and the maldistribution of the nation's wealth and services." Finally, at the behest of Nancy Hardesty, professor of English at Trinity College (Deerfield, Illinois), the declaration reaffirmed evangelicalism's commitment to women's equality.[10]

One of the Christians who quickly endorsed the Chicago Declaration was Mark O. Hatfield, US senator from Oregon, a Republican. While serving as Oregon governor and prior to his election to the Senate in 1966, Hatfield was the lone governor who voted against a resolution supporting Lyndon Johnson's prosecution of the war in Vietnam. In 1970 Hatfield joined George S. McGovern, Democratic senator from South Dakota, erstwhile ministerial student at Garrett Theological Seminary, and a Methodist profoundly shaped by the Social Gospel, to sponsor the McGovern–Hatfield Amendment to End the War in Vietnam. Hatfield, a devout Baptist, doggedly defended the separation of church and state throughout his political career.[11]

Another Baptist, Jimmy Carter, entered the national scene in the 1970s. Elected governor of Georgia in 1970, Carter announced his candidacy for president on December 12, 1974, promising, in the wake of the Watergate scandal, that he would "never knowingly lie" to the American people. No one has credibly accused him of breaking that pledge during his four years in the White House. Because he served only one term, much of Carter's agenda was unfinished, which helps to explain the remarkable energy he devoted to his post-presidency. Carter nevertheless sought to govern according to his religious scruples, even as he assiduously respected the line of separation between church and state.

Carter sought to shift American foreign policy away from the reflexive dualism of the Cold War and toward an emphasis on human rights, a policy that angered many allies but also prompted the release of political prisoners. He recognized that if the United States were to have any meaningful relationship with Third World nations, especially those in Latin America, we needed to temper our colonialist policies.

At great political cost, therefore, Carter pushed for the revision and ratification of the Panama Canal treaties. He advocated for peace in the Middle East, and his success in securing the Camp David Accords advanced that process more than any previous—or successive—president. Carter appointed more women and people of color than any previous president, and many environmentalists consider him the best environmental president ever.

One need not approve of Carter's policies or his presidency to appreciate his integrity and the sincerity of his Christian convictions, especially as demonstrated by his humanitarian work after he left the White House. At the final cabinet meeting of Carter's presidency, after he had lost his bid for reelection, Carter asked cabinet members to summarize their accomplishments. Walter Mondale, Carter's vice president, went last. "We told the truth. We obeyed the law. We kept the peace," Mondale said. "And that ain't bad."[12]

The peril of including more recent examples of Christian faithfulness is that they haven't stood the test of time. History has a way of separating the sheep from the goats, to use a biblical metaphor, and it's entirely possible that those who appear faithful, even heroic, today may suffer a lapse at some point, or some sordid, questionable action might come to light.

With that caveat, and acknowledging once again our shared humanity and imperfections, let me offer a few more recent examples who may be worthy of emulation if the Christian faith is to be rehabilitated in the twenty-first century. For decades I have looked to Jim Wallis, founder of Sojourners, for inspiration and for consistent advocacy for social justice. In 2021 Wallis stepped away from Sojourners to direct the Center on Faith and Justice at Georgetown University, thereby finding a new arena for his Christian activism. Others in the cohort pushing for social justice would include Peggy and Tony Campolo, Shane Claiborne, Lisa Sharon Harper, Jemar Tisby, and many others. William J. Barber II led Moral Mondays beginning in 2013 to protest the North Carolina governor and legislature's regressive laws and policies directed against voting access and people of color. Raphael Warnock, a graduate of Union Theological Seminary in New York City and pastor of Ebenezer Baptist Church in Atlanta, brought his Christian convictions and the mandate for social justice to Washington following his election to the United States Senate in 2021.

Early in 2022 David Brooks, conservative columnist for the *New York Times*, produced a piece, "The Dissenters Trying to Save Evangelicalism from Itself," in which he profiled those who were attempting to rescue evangelicalism from the cult of Donald Trump and other heresies. Brooks praised the efforts of Beth Moore, who left the Southern Baptist Convention over its continued embrace of Trump and its refusal to confront sexual abuse scandals within the denomination. Brooks highlighted the efforts of various individuals who have dedicated themselves to racial reconciliation and mentioned Walter

Kim, head of the National Association of Evangelicals, and Karen Swallow Prior, formerly a defender of Jerry Falwell Jr. and Liberty University, who are pushing for reforms as well.[13]

Brooks ended his column on a note of hope. "Hints of Christian renewal are becoming visible," he wrote.[14]

7

THE CASE FOR
PROPHETIC CHRISTIANITY

. . . if my people, who are called by my name, will humble themselves and pray and seek my face and turn from their wicked ways, then I will hear from heaven, and I will forgive their sin and will heal their land.

—2 Chronicles 7:14

AS A HISTORIAN of religion in North America, I've long argued that the most vibrant religious movements in American history have positioned themselves at the margins of society rather than in the councils of power. Conversely, once a religion begins to lust after political or cultural influence, it loses its energy—as well as its prophetic voice.

Sadly, that describes American Christianity over the past half century or so. In their hunger for power, Christian leaders have lost their tradition's once robust prophetic voice. Let me illustrate. When I was growing up within the evangelical subculture in the middle decades of the twentieth century, we understood ourselves as a counterculture. We stood at arm's length from the broader culture, which our parents assured us was both corrupt and corrupting. The most damning thing you could say about a fellow believer was that she was "worldly." The label "worldliness" could take many forms—sexual promiscuity, drinking, drugs, dancing—but one of the defining characteristics of our evangelical counterculture was a suspicion of affluence.

More recently, in the age of the Religious Right, evangelicalism still bears the marks of a subculture; it has its own music, vocabulary, mores, and celebrities. But evangelicalism is no longer a counterculture. In its quest for political power and culture influence, it has lost its prophetic voice. It has become worldly. Put another way, I heard a lot of sermons about camels negotiating the eyes of needles when I was growing up evangelical, a reference to Jesus's declaration that "it is easier for a camel to go through the eye of a needle than for someone who is rich to enter the kingdom of God." I haven't heard any such sermon in decades.[1]

Part of our condemnation of affluence in the middle decades of the twentieth century was due no doubt to the fact that we coveted it, although few of my evangelical contemporaries would have admitted such a thing. The failure in recent years lies not so much in the pursuit of middle-class comforts, or even wealth itself, but the refusal to denounce what Maureen Dowd calls "the corrosive effect of our culture of greed, selfishness and billionaires"—and even worse, the "baptism" of acquisitiveness.[2]

How did Christianity in America veer away from New Testament teachings and nineteenth-century condemnations of affluence to an embrace of free-market capitalism? Much of the impetus can be traced to an opposition to Franklin Roosevelt's New Deal and suspicions of communism. James W. Fifield Jr., for instance, pastor of First Congregational Church in Los Angeles, opponent of the New Deal, and founder of a movement called Spiritual Mobilization, assured his affluent followers that "the blessings of capitalism come from God." A 1952 letter from the head of the Committee Against Socialist Housing congratulated Fifield, known as Apostle to the Millionaires, for his "militant leadership in behalf of free enterprise and American individualism." Lyman Stewart, of Union Oil Company, and J. Howard Pew, of Sun Oil Company and ally of Billy Graham, believed that Christianity and capitalism were intertwined, despite the fact that Charles Grandison Finney and other evangelicals in the nineteenth century averred that a "Christian businessman" was an oxymoron because capitalism elevated avarice over altruism.[3]

But the real push occurred later. In addition to the prosperity preachers, Jerry Falwell and other televangelists picked up on the supposed link between faith and riches; Falwell famously declared that material wealth is "God's way of blessing people." I've long believed that the so-called prosperity gospel flourished coincident with the trickle-down economics of the Reagan era. Prosperity teachings represented a kind of spiritualized Reaganism, where "showers of blessing" would trickle down to the faithful—albeit only after they had cycled through the rain barrel of the televangelists and the prosperity preachers themselves.

If prophetic Christianity is to regain a toehold in American society, we must take a sober look at the "worldliness" that has infected Christianity in America—not only the distortions wrought by the Religious Right, but also the cultural captivity of mainline Protestantism and the craven embrace of Trumpism by members of the American Catholic hierarchy. We must pay renewed attention to the maldistribution of resources, the growing chasm between rich and poor, both in the United States and around the world. We must exorcise the demons of racism and American nationalism. We must step outside of the power structures to recover a prophetic voice. We must look anew at the Scriptures, not as a cudgel to wield against our supposed enemies but as a guide for daily living and a template for how we treat others. We must reaffiliate with the best of our past, and we must recover the tradition of prophetic Christianity.

Let's begin with the Bible. As an evangelical, I grew up hearing the phrase "Word of God" used synonymously with the Bible. "Let's turn to the Word of God," the preacher or televangelist would say as he riffled through the pages of his well-thumbed Bible. Make no mistake, I believe that the Scriptures are God's revelation to humanity. But I was well into my sixties before I realized that the Bible was far too narrow a definition for the term "Word of God."

As I suggested earlier, if we read carefully the first chapter of John's Gospel, the "Word of God" is Jesus. "In the beginning was the Word, and the Word was with God, and the Word was God," John writes. "He was with God in the beginning. Through him all things were made; without him nothing was made that has been made. In him was life, and that life was the light of all mankind. The light shines in the darkness, and the darkness has not overcome it."[4]

If we take the Scriptures seriously, as all Christians should, then we see that *Jesus* is the Word of God. And if we understand Jesus as the Word of God, then we as his followers are compelled to honor his teachings and to emulate his example. That entails a respect for the Hebrew Prophets and their calls for justice—Jesus was clear that he came not to abolish the law or the prophets, but to fulfill them—but it also entails treating others, especially women and foreigners and cultural outcasts, as Jesus did, with compassion.[5]

This more capacious understanding of the "Word of God" as Jesus and not merely the Bible should at the very least temper the impulse to bludgeon others with proof texts, especially those wrenched out of context. Jesus did not do that, and neither should his followers.

Douglas Frank, drawing on the work of French Catholic thinker Jean Sulivan, talks about the paradoxes surrounding Jesus himself, who captivated crowds, albeit not for the purpose of deception or for political ends. Jesus understood the power of propaganda, but he used it not for his own aggrandizement, but to empower individuals to act on their own behalf. Christianity itself is countercultural, a religion riddled with paradoxes. A baby born to immigrant parents in a stable was the progenitor of a faith that upended the world. Jesus declared that "whoever would save his life will lose it, but whoever loses his life for my sake will find it." St. Paul insisted that he had been told by the Lord that "my power is made perfect in weakness." Christianity, a countercultural faith, is most prophetic outside the councils of power.[6]

The words of Martin Luther King Jr. bear repeating here. "The church must be reminded that it is not the master or the servant of the state, but rather the conscience of the state," King said. "It must be the guide and the critic of the state, and never its tool. If the church does not recapture its prophetic zeal, it will become an irrelevant social club without moral or spiritual authority."[7]

What might prophetic Christianity look like in the twenty-first century? I suspect it would focus on the matter of justice, for that is the issue that preoccupied the Hebrew Prophets, animated the teachings of Jesus, and informed Christian social activism in the nineteenth and early twentieth centuries. Justice for whom? The poor, certainly, because Jesus told his followers to care for "the least of these." He also told us to welcome the stranger and visit the prisoner, and his demeanor toward cultural outcasts—foreigners, the sick and the lame, women in his patriarchal society—suggests compassion and empathy rather than condemnation. Nowhere in the Gospels do we find Jesus, the Word of God, treating women with condescension.

Prophetic Christianity would be less interested in building walls than constructing bridges. It would be less concerned with banning books than with appropriating consistently the teachings of Jesus. Prophetic Christians care about truth and truth-telling, even when truth is inconvenient and riles those in power. And who can fail to appreciate the irony of so-called Christian nationalists hankering to post the Ten Commandments in public places and simultaneously lionizing a politician who, according to independent sources, issued well over thirty thousand false or misleading statements over the course of his four-year presidency, an average of twenty-one a day? One of those commandments reads, "You shall not bear false witness against your neighbor."[8]

Prophetic Christianity in the twenty-first century must surely address the ravages of climate change, the proliferation of plastics, the grotesque inhumanity of factory farms, the destruction of ancient forests, and environmental degradation. If we truly believe that the created order is God's handiwork, then we bear responsibility for its protection.

Prophetic Christianity, by definition, is countercultural. It stands against the values of the broader society, especially avarice. The growing chasm between rich and poor, those with access to medical care and those without, would be a scandal in any society, but even more so in a nation whose citizens claim to be Christian. Charles Grandison Finney and others recognized that long ago. Perhaps it's time once again for a sermon or two about camels and the eye of a needle.

Finally, if Christians acknowledge Jesus as the Word of God, we must come to terms with the suffering servant, the man of sorrows acquainted with grief, suspended on a cross between heaven and earth. His body was bruised and broken. There's nothing triumphant about that image; it's certainly not a summons to Christian nationalism.

If we identify once again with the sufferings of Jesus, the Word of God, I suspect we'll find it a tad more difficult to discriminate against others because of religion, race, gender, immigration status, or sexual identity—or anything else we conjure to demean or diminish others. Instead, we might recognize and even identify with their sufferings, see in them another child of God rather than a deviant. The suffering servant suspended on a cross looks a lot more to me like Matthew Shepard pinned to a barbed-wire fence on a cold Wyoming night than it resembles his tormenters. The man of sorrows, the Word of God, understands and looks with compassion upon the refugee family detained at the border and the Black teenager living in fear of an encounter with the police.

Prophetic Christianity positions itself at the margins. It calls the powerful to account, and it identifies with those Jesus called "the least of these." And that brings us very close to the gospel, the "good news."

It sounds to me like good news indeed.

APPENDIX

Chicago Declaration of Evangelical Social Concern

As evangelical Christians committed to the Lord Jesus Christ and the full authority of the Word of God, we affirm that God lays total claim upon the lives of his people. We cannot, therefore, separate our lives from the situation in which God has placed us in the United States and the world.

We confess that we have not acknowledged the complete claim of God on our lives.

We acknowledge that God requires love. But we have not demonstrated the love of God to those suffering social abuses.

We acknowledge that God requires justice. But we have not proclaimed or demonstrated his justice to an unjust American society. Although the Lord calls us to defend the social and economic rights of the poor and oppressed, we have mostly remained silent. We deplore the historic involvement of the church in America with racism and the conspicuous responsibility of the evangelical community for perpetuating the personal attitudes and institutional structures that have divided the body of Christ along color lines. Further, we have failed to condemn the exploitation of racism at home and abroad by our economic system.

We affirm that God abounds in mercy and that he forgives all who repent and turn from their sins. So we call our fellow evangelical Christians to demonstrate repentance in a Christian discipleship that confronts the social and political injustice of our nation.

We must attack the materialism of our culture and the maldistribution of the nation's wealth and services. We recognize that as a nation we play a crucial role in the imbalance and injustice of international trade and development. Before God and a billion hungry neighbors, we must rethink our values regarding our present standard of living and promote a more just acquisition and distribution of the world's resources.

We acknowledge our Christian responsibilities of citizenship. Therefore, we must challenge the misplaced trust of the nation in economic and military might—a proud trust that promotes a national pathology of war and violence which victimizes our neighbors at home and abroad. We must resist the temptation to make the nation and its institutions objects of near-religious loyalty.

We acknowledge that we have encouraged men to prideful domination and women to irresponsible passivity. So we call both men and women to mutual submission and active discipleship.

We proclaim no new gospel, but the Gospel of our Lord Jesus Christ who, through the power of the Holy Spirit, frees people from sin so that they might praise God through works of righteousness.

By this declaration, we endorse no political ideology or party, but call our nation's leaders and people to that righteousness which exalts a nation.

We make this declaration in the biblical hope that Christ is coming to consummate the Kingdom and we accept his claim on our total discipleship until he comes.

November 25, 1973
Chicago, Illinois

NOTES

Chapter 1

1 Yonat Shimron, "More Americans Are Becoming Secular, Poll Says," *Washington Post*, December 17, 2021.

2 Shimron, "More Americans Are Becoming Secular."

3 Quoted in Shimron, "More Americans Are Becoming Secular."

4 David A. Hollinger, *After Cloven Tongues of Fire: Protestant Liberalism in Modern American History* (Princeton, NJ: Princeton University Press, 2013), chap. 2, quote on 18.

5 Randall Balmer, *Grant Us Courage: Travels along the Mainline of American Protestantism* (New York: Oxford University Press, 1996), chap. 3.

6 David A. Hollinger, *Christianity's American Fate: How Religion Became More Conservative and Society More Secular* (Princeton, NJ: Princeton University Press, 2022).

7 Balmer, *Grant Us Courage*, 147.

8 For a quick summary of my views on ecumenism, see "United We Fall," *New York Times*, August 28, 1999, A25.

9 I have addressed this issue far more thoroughly—and with copious footnotes—in *Bad Faith: Race and the*

Rise of the Religious Right (Grand Rapids, MI: Wm. B. Eerdmans, 2021).

10 Randall Balmer, *Redeemer: The Life of Jimmy Carter* (New York: Basic Books, 2014).

11 The following book was enormously helpful in my reexamination of Reagan: Daniel S. Lucks, *Reconsidering Reagan: Racism, Republicans, and the Road to Trump* (Boston: Beacon Press, 2020). See also Sam Kleiner, "Apartheid Amnesia: How the GOP Conveniently Forgot about Its Role in Propping Up a White Supremacist Regime," *Foreign Policy*, July 19, 2013.

12 Regarding Moore and Perkins, see Balmer, *Bad Faith*, 75–76.

13 Quoted in Randall Balmer, "Catholics Are Questioning Biden?" *Los Angeles Times*, November 23, 2020, A11. In addition to the Catholic bishops' threatening Biden with excommunication, the archbishop of San Francisco, Salvatore Cordileone, barred Nancy Pelosi, speaker of the House of Representatives, in May 2022.

Chapter 2

1 Emily Yahr, "How Ted Koppel's Trip to 'Mayberry' Turned into One of 2021's Most Striking Moments of TV," *Washington Post*, December 29, 2021. The quotes are taken from the video link to the original broadcast.

2 Sidney E. Mead, *The Lively Experiment: The Shaping of Christianity in America* (New York: Harper & Row, 1963).

3 Quoted in Kermit L. Hall, ed., *The Supreme Court in American Society: Equal Justice under Law* (New York: Garland Publishing, 2001), 1479.

4 Alexis de Tocqueville, *Democracy in America* (New York: Library of America, 2004), 341.

5 Roger Williams, *The Bloudy Tenent of Persecution for Conscience Discussed* (London: J. Haddon, 1848), xxv.

6 Williams, *Bloudy Tenent*, 435.

7 Quoted in Kathryn Jean Lopez, "The Church Must Be the Conscience of the State," *National Review*, January 25, 2021.

Chapter 3

1 Quoted in John Ghazvinian and Arthur Mitchell Fraas, eds., *American and Muslims Worlds before 1900* (New York: Bloomsbury Academic, 2020), 10; letter, George Washington to Edward Newenham, October 20, 1792, in Jared Sparks, *The Writings of George Washington; Being His Correspondence, Addresses, Messages, and Other Papers, Official and Private*, vol. 12 (Boston, 1837), 404–405.

2 Quoted in J. David Hoeveler, *Creating the American Mind: Intellect and Politics in the Colonial Colleges* (Lanham, MD: Rowman & Littlefield, 2007), 310; quoted in Daniel Dreisbach, Mark D. Hall, and Jeffry H. Morrison, eds., *The Founders on God and Government* (Lanham, MD: Rowman & Littlefield, 2004), 234; quoted in Jeffry Hays Morrison, "John Witherspoon and 'The Public Interest of Religion,'" *Journal of Church and State* 41 (Summer 1999): 551.

3 Letter from John Adams to Abigail Adams, 28 January 1799 (electronic edition), *Adams Family Papers: An Electronic Archive*, Massachusetts Historical Society, http://www.masshist.org/digitaladams/; letter from John Adams to Benjamin Rush, April 18, 1808, https://

founders.archives.gov/documents/Adams/99-02-02-5238; James H. Hutson, ed., *The Founders on Religion: A Book of Quotations* (Princeton, NJ: Princeton University Press, 2005), 121.

4 Walter Isaacson, ed., *A Benjamin Franklin Reader* (New York: Simon & Schuster, 2003), 106; quoted in James Madison Stifler, *The Religion of Benjamin Franklin* (New York: D. Appleton & Co., 1925), 34.

5 Franklin Bowditch Dexter, ed., *The Literary Diary of Ezra Stiles, D.D., LL.D.*, vol. 3 (New York: Charles Scribner's Sons, 1901), 387.

6 Quoted in John McCollister, *Echoes from the Smithsonian: America's History Brought to Life* (Champaign, IL: Spotlight Press, 2004), 175.

7 Thomas Fitzhugh, ed., *Letters of Thomas Jefferson Concerning Philology and the Classics* (Charlottesville: University of Virginia, 1919), 33; quoted in Stephen J. Vicchio, *Jefferson's Religion* (Eugene, OR: Wipf & Stock, 2007), 112; quoted in Garry Wills, *Under God: Religion and American Politics* (New York: Simon & Schuster, 1990), 358.

8 Quoted in Martha C. Nussbaum, *Liberty of Conscience: In Defense of America's Tradition of Religious Equality* (New York: Basic Books, 2008), 89; quoted in Ralph L. Ketcham, "James Madison and Religion—A New Hypothesis," *Journal of the Presbyterian Historical Society* 38 (June 1960): 66.

9 Regarding the Treaty of Tripoli, see Randall Balmer, *Solemn Reverence: The Separation of Church and State in American Life* (Hanover, NH: Steerforth Press, 2021), chap. 5.

Chapter 4

1 Quoted in Philip Weeks, *"Farewell, My Nation": American Indians and the United States in the Nineteenth Century*, 3rd ed. (Oxford: Wiley Blackwell, 2016), 143.

2 David Wallace Adams, *Education for Extinction: American Indians and the Boarding School Experience, 1875–1928* (Lawrence: University Press of Kansas, 1995), 27.

3 The particular references are Genesis 9:25; Philemon; Colossians 3:22; Ephesians 6:5–6; Galatians 3:28. Titus 2:9–10 and 1 Peter 2:18–19 were also used to justify slavery.

4 James Henley Thornwell, *The State of the Country: An Article Republished from the Southern Presbyterian Review* (Columbia, SC: Southern Guardian Steam-Powered Press, 1860), 12, 13; James Henley Thornwell, *The Collected Writings of James Henley Thornwell, D.D., LL.D.*, ed. John B. Adger and John L. Girardeau (Richmond: Presbyterian Committee of Publication, 1873), 460. See also Marilyn J. Westerkamp, "James Henley Thornwell, Pro-Slavery Spokesman within a Calvinist Faith," *South Carolina Historical Magazine* 87 (January 1986): 49–64; Mark A. Noll, "Theology, Presbyterian History, and the Civil War," *Journal of Presbyterian History* 89 (Spring/Summer 2011): 4–15.

5 Robert L. Dabney, *A Defence of Virginia, and through Her, of the South, in Recent and Pending Contests against the Sectional Party* (New York: E. J. Hale & Son, 1867), 195, 280, 281–282. See also Mark A. Noll, *The Civil War as a Theological Crisis* (Chapel Hill: University of North Carolina Press, 2006).

6 Joseph Bell, "A Catholic Proslavery Perspective," MA thesis, California State University, Chico, Spring 2013.

7 William Joseph Simmons, "The Ku Klux Klan: Yesterday, Today and Forever," pamphlet, ca. 1916; Charles O. Jackson, "William J. Simmons: A Career in Ku Kluxism," *Georgia Historical Society* 50 (December 1966): 351–365.

8 Linda Gordon, *The Second Coming of the KKK: The Ku Klux Klan of the 1920s and the American Political Tradition* (New York: Liveright, 2017), 186, 90, 91.

9 Southern Poverty Law Center website: https://www.splcenter.org/fighting-hate/extremist-files/individual/peter-brimelow, accessed February 2, 2022. In the interest of full disclosure, I must reveal that Brimelow occasionally showed up in my parish when I was rector of St. John's Episcopal Church in Washington, Connecticut. I was unaware of his views at the time.

Chapter 5

1 John 1:1.

2 The best treatment of the Scopes Trial is Edward J. Larson, *Summer for the Gods: The Scopes Trial and America's Continuing Debate over Science and Religion* (New York: Basic Books, 2006). On intelligent design, see Edward Humes, *Monkey Girl: Education, Religion, and the Battle for America's Soul* (New York: HarperCollins, 2007); Randall Balmer, *Thy Kingdom Come: How the Religious Right Distorts the Faith and Threatens America* (New York: Basic Books, 2006), chap. 4.

3 The texts addressing same-sex relationships are Leviticus 18:22 and 20:13; mixed fabrics: 19:19. The infectious disease chapters are Leviticus 13–14.

4 Leviticus 19:34.

5 Exodus 23:6; Deuteronomy 27:19: Proverbs 29:7, 21:5.

6 Isaiah 1:17; Jeremiah 5:28; Ezekiel 22:29; Amos 5:15; Zechariah 7:9.

7 Luke 4:18–19; Matthew 23:23.

8 Matthew 25:40, 35–36.

9 Jesus did, however, have something to say about divorce, none of it good.

Chapter 6

1 Ann M. Burton, "British Evangelicals, Economic Warfare and the Abolition of the Atlantic Slave Trade, 1794–1810," *Anglican and Episcopal History* 65 (June 1996): 197–225, quote on 225; Stephen Tomkins, *William Wilberforce: A Biography* (Grand Rapids, MI: Wm. B. Eerdmans, 2007).

2 Harry S. Stout, *The Divine Dramatist: George Whitefield and the Rise of Modern Evangelicalism* (Grand Rapids, MI: Wm. B. Eerdmans, 1991); George M. Marsden, *Jonathan Edwards: A Life* (New Haven, CT: Yale University Press, 2003).

3 C. C. Foote, "Woman's Rights and Duties," *Oberlin Quarterly Review* 4 (October 1849): 383, 406–407, 396. See also Margaret Hope Bacon, *Mothers of Feminism: The Story of Quaker Women in America* (New York: HarperCollins, 1986).

4 "Thoughts on the Importance and Improvement of Common Schools," *Christian Spectator* n.s., 1 (February 1827): 85; James E. Pilcher, *Life and Labors of Elijah H. Pilcher of Michigan: Fifty-Nine Years as Minister of the Methodist Episcopal Church* (New York, 1892), 106, 118, 89, 116–117.

5 Charles G. Finney, *Sermons on Gospel Themes* (Oberlin, OH: E. J. Goodrich, 1876), 348, 356.

6 Finney, *Sermons on Gospel Themes*, 352, 354. Finney upheld Bible societies as business models. On Roman Catholic attitudes toward affluence and, especially, private property, see E. Brooks Holifield, *Theology in America: Christian Thought from the Age of the Puritans to the Civil War* (New Haven, CT: Yale University Press, 2003), 418.

7 "The Farmer in Hard Times," *New-York Evangelist*, July 22, 1837, 118; "Stewardship of Wealth," *New-York Evangelist*, January 2, 1836, 1; "Reflections on Wealth," *Christian Chronicle*, November 7, 1818, 314.

8 Quoted in Kenneth L. Woodward, "A $1 Million Habit," *Newsweek*, September 15, 1980, 35.

9 Regarding Perkins, see Randall Balmer, *Mine Eyes Have Seen the Glory: A Journey into the Evangelical Subculture in America*, 5th ed. (New York: Oxford University Press, 2014), chap. 9.

10 The Chicago Declaration of 1973 is reproduced in the Appendix to this volume.

11 On McGovern's religious views, see Thomas J. Knock, *The Life and Times of George McGovern: The Rise of a Prairie Statesman* (Princeton, NJ: Princeton University Press, 2016), 82–84.

12 Quoted in Balmer, *Redeemer: The Life of Jimmy Carter*, 156.

13 David Brooks, "The Dissenters Trying to Save Evangelicalism from Itself," *New York Times*, February 4, 2002.

14 Brooks, "Dissenters."

Chapter 7

1 Matthew 19:24.

2 Maureen Dowd, "Zelensky Answers Hamlet," *New York Times*, March 13, 2022, SR9.

3 Eckard V. Toy Jr., "Spiritual Mobilization: The Failure of an Ultraconservative Ideal in the 1950s," *Pacific Northwest Quarterly* 61 (April 1970): 77–86, quote on 77; B. M. Pietsch, "Lyman Stewart and Early Fundamentalism," *Church History* 82 (September 2013): 617–646; letter from Frederick C. Dockweiler to James W. Fifield Jr., April 17, 1952, Dockweiler Family Papers, William H. Hannon Library, Loyola Marymount University. On Fifield, see Kevin M. Kruse, *One Nation under God: How Corporate America Invented Christian America* (New York: Basic Books, 2015), chap. 1.

4 John 1:1–5.

5 Matthew 5:17.

6 Doug Frank, *A Gentler God: Breaking Free of the Almighty in the Company of the Human Jesus* (Eugene, OR: Wipf & Stock, 2020), 189; Matthew 16:25 (ESV); 2 Corinthians 12:9.

7 Quoted in Lopez, "The Church Must Be the Conscience of the State."

8 Glenn Kessler, Salvador Rizzo, and Meg Kelly, "Trump's False or Misleading Claims Total 30,573 over 4 Years," *Washington Post*, January 24, 2021; Exodus 20:16 (ESV).

SELECTED BIBLIOGRAPHY

Balmer, Randall. *Bad Faith: Race and the Rise of the Religious Right*. Grand Rapids, MI: Wm. B. Eerdmans, 2021.

_____. *Grant Us Courage: Travels along the Mainline of American Protestantism*. New York: Oxford University Press, 1996.

_____. *Mine Eyes Have Seen the Glory: A Journey into the Evangelical Subculture in America*, 5th ed. New York: Oxford University Press, 2014.

_____. *Redeemer: The Life of Jimmy Carter*. New York: Basic Books, 2014.

Butler, Anthea. *White Evangelical Racism: The Politics of Morality in America*. Chapel Hill: University of North Carolina Press, 2021.

Carter, Heath. *Union Made: Working People and the Rise of Social Christianity in Chicago*. New York: Oxford University Press, 2015.

Chaves, Mark. *American Religion: Contemporary Trends*, 2nd ed. Princeton, NJ: Princeton University Press, 2017.

Collins, John. *What Are Biblical Values? What the Bible Says on Key Ethical Issues*. New Haven, CT: Yale University Press, 2019.

Dionne, E. J., Jr. *Code Red: How Progressives and Moderates Can Unite to Save Our Country*. New York: St. Martin's Press, 2020.

Du Mez, Kristen Kobes. *Jesus and John Wayne: How White Evangelicals Corrupted a Faith and Fractured a Nation*. New York: Liveright, 2020.

Fea, John. *Believe Me: The Evangelical Road to Donald Trump*. Grand Rapids, MI: Wm. B. Eerdmans, 2020.

Frank, Doug. *A Gentler God: Breaking Free of the Almighty in the Company of the Human Jesus.* Eugene, OR: Wipf & Stock, 2020.

Gilgoff, Dan. *The Jesus Machine: How James Dobson, Focus on the Family, and Evangelical America Are Winning the Culture War.* New York: St. Martin's Press, 2007.

Glaude, Eddie S., Jr. *Democracy in Black: How Race Still Enslaves the American Soul.* New York: Crown, 2017.

Gorski, Philip S., and Samuel L. Perry. *The Flag and the Cross: White Christian Nationalism and the Threat to American Democracy.* Foreword by Jemar Tisby. New York: Oxford University Press, 2022.

Green, Steven K. *Separating Church and State: A History.* Ithaca, NY: Cornell University Press, 2022.

Hardesty, Nancy A. *Women Called to Witness: Evangelical Feminism in the Nineteenth Century,* 2nd ed. Knoxville: University of Tennessee Press, 1999.

Harper, Lisa Sharon. *Evangelical Does Not Equal Republican or Democrat.* Foreword by John M. Perkins. New York: New Press, 2008.

———. *The Very Good Gospel: How Everything Wrong Can Be Made Right.* Foreword by Walter Brueggemann. Colorado Springs: WaterBrook & Multnomah, 2016.

Hawkins, J. Russell. *The Bible Told Them So: How Southern Evangelicals Fought to Preserve White Supremacy.* New York: Oxford University Press, 2021.

Hendricks, Obery M., Jr. *Christians against Christianity: How Right-Wing Evangelicals Are Destroying Our Nation and Our Faith.* Boston: Beacon Press, 2021.

Hollinger, David A. *After Cloven Tongues of Fire: Protestant Liberalism in Modern American History.* Princeton, NJ: Princeton University Press, 2013.

———. *Christianity's American Fate: How Religion Became More Conservative and Society More Secular.* Princeton, NJ: Princeton University Press, 2022.

Ingersoll, Julie J. *Building God's Kingdom: Inside the World of Christian Reconstruction*. New York: Oxford University Press, 2015.

Jennings, Willie James. *The Christian Imagination: Theology and the Origins of Race*. New Haven, CT: Yale University Press, 2011.

Jones, Robert P. *White Too Long: The Legacy of White Supremacy in American Christianity*. New York: Simon & Schuster, 2020.

Keddie, Tony. *Republican Jesus: How the Right Has Rewritten the Gospels*. Berkeley and Los Angeles: University of California Press, 2020.

Lucks, Daniel S. *Reconsidering Reagan: Racism, Republicans, and the Road to Trump*. Boston: Beacon Press, 2020.

Marsh, Charles. *God's Long Summer: Stories of Faith and Civil Rights*. Princeton, NJ: Princeton University Press, 1997.

Marshall, Jermaine. *Christianity Corrupted: The Scandal of White Supremacy*. Foreword by William J. Barber II. Maryknoll, NY: Orbis Books, 2021.

Martin, William. *With God on Our Side: The Rise of the Religious Right in America*. New York: Broadway Books, 1996.

Moore, Andrew S., ed. *Evangelicals and Presidential Politics: From Jimmy Carter to Donald Trump*. Baton Rouge: Louisiana State University Press, 2021.

Nelson, Anne. *Shadow Network: Media, Money, and the Secret Hub of the Radical Right*. New York: Bloomsbury, 2019.

Patel, Eboo. *Sacred Ground: Pluralism, Prejudice, and the Promise of America*. Boston: Beacon Press, 2012.

Posner, Sarah. *Unholy: Why White Evangelicals Worship at the Altar of Donald Trump*. New York: Random House, 2020.

Raboteau, Albert J. *American Prophets: Seven Religious Radicals and Their Struggle for Social and Political Justice*. Princeton, NJ: Princeton University Press, 2016.

Rah, Soon-Chan. *Prophetic Lament: A Call for Justice in Troubled Times*. Foreword by Brenda Salter McNeil. Downers Grove, IL: Inter-Varsity Press, 2015.

Schaeffer, Frank. *Crazy for God: How I Grew Up as One of the Elect, Helped Found the Religious Right, and Lived to Take All (or Almost All) of It Back.* New York: Carroll & Graf, 2007.

Schulman, Bruce J., and Julian E. Zelizer, eds. *Rightward Bound: Making America Conservative in the 1970s.* Cambridge, MA: Harvard University Press, 2008.

Scully, Matthew. *Dominion: The Power of Man, the Suffering of Animals, and the Call to Mercy.* New York: St. Martin's Griffin, 2002.

Sider, Ronald J. *Rich Christians in an Age of Hunger: Moving from Affluence to Generosity,* 6th ed. Nashville: Thomas Nelson, 2015.

_____, ed. *The Spiritual Danger of Donald Trump: 30 Evangelical Christians on Justice, Truth, and Moral Integrity.* Eugene, OR: Cascade Books, 2020.

Stevens, Stuart. *It Was All a Lie: How the Republican Party Became Donald Trump.* New York: Alfred A. Knopf, 2020.

Stewart, Katherine. *The Power Worshippers: Inside the Dangerous Rise of Religious Nationalism.* New York: Bloomsbury, 2020.

Stout, Jeffrey. *Democracy and Tradition,* rev. ed. Princeton, NJ: Princeton University Press, 2004.

Swartz, David R. *Moral Minority: The Evangelical Left in an Age of Conservatism.* Philadelphia: University of Pennsylvania Press, 2012.

Taylor, Adam Russell. *A More Perfect Union: A New Vision for Building the Beloved Community.* Foreword by John Lewis. Minneapolis: Broadleaf Books, 2021.

Thomas, Cal, and Ed Dobson. *Blinded by Might: Can the Religious Right Save America?* Grand Rapids, MI: Zondervan, 1999.

Vaca, Daniel. *Evangelicals Incorporated: Books and the Business of Religion in America.* Cambridge, MA: Harvard University Press, 2019.

Wallis, Jim. *America's Original Sin: Racism, White Privilege, and the Bridge to a New America.* Foreword by Bryan Stevenson. Grand Rapids, MI: Brazos Press, 2016.

West, Cornel. *Race Matters*. Boston: Beacon Press, 2017.

Whitehead, Andrew L., and Samuel L. Perry. *Taking America Back for God: Christian Nationalism in the United States*. New York: Oxford University Press, 2020.

Williams, Clifford. *The Uneasy Conscience of a White Christian: Making Racial Equity a Priority*. Eugene, OR: Wipf & Stock, 2021.

Williams, Daniel K. *Defenders of the Unborn: The Pro-Life Movement before* Roe v. Wade. New York: Oxford University Press, 2016.

————. *God's Own Party: The Making of the Christian Right*. New York: Oxford University Press, 2012.

Winters, Michael Sean. *God's Right Hand: How Jerry Falwell Made God a Republican and Baptized the American Right*. San Francisco: HarperOne, 2012.

Ziegler, Mary. *Abortion and the Law in America:* Roe v. Wade *to the Present*. Cambridge: Cambridge University Press, 2020.

ACKNOWLEDGMENTS

In the fall of 1975, my senior year in college, I was one of twenty-two students and five faculty who participated in an extension program in the Cascade Mountains of southern Oregon. Sponsored by my undergraduate institution, Trinity College, in Deerfield, Illinois, and located in a former logging camp between Ashland and Klamath Falls, the Oregon Extension combined rigorous academic pursuits with wilderness excursions, all in the context of community. We read books, discussed ideas, shared meals and occasionally a song or two. It was there I learned to think critically and question fearlessly.

I had been at best an indifferent student to that point, coasting on a modicum of intelligence but rarely testing its limits. But the organizers of the Oregon Extension, especially Douglas Frank and Sam Alvord, apparently saw something in me that I didn't yet recognize in myself. I've rarely been the smartest guy in the room, then or since, but once I tasted the delights of scholarship, it changed the trajectory of my life.

I decided early in the writing of this book, therefore, that I would dedicate it to Doug Frank and Sam Alvord in gratitude for providing that environment and for their counterintuitive confidence in me. As it happened, Doug and

I engaged in one of our occasional email exchanges while this manuscript was in gestation. One thing led to another, and he agreed to cast his eye once again on something I had written. This book is better for his critical insights, although I alone bear responsibility for its contents.

One final note. I'm often credited for the currency of the term "subculture" to describe the vast and tangled brocade of evangelical institutions, mores, and folkways; I used the term in the subtitle of my second book, *Mine Eyes Have Seen the Glory*, and countless times thereafter. However, here is a good place to set the record straight: I first heard the term "evangelical subculture" from Doug Frank when I was an undergraduate at Trinity College.

No one appreciates better than he the importance of historical accuracy.

Hanover, New Hampshire
Day of Pentecost
June 5, 2022

ABOUT THE AUTHOR

Randall Balmer is the John Phillips Professor in Religion at Dartmouth College, the oldest endowed chair at the college. After earning his PhD from Princeton University and before coming to Dartmouth in 2012, he was Professor of North American Religions at Columbia University for twenty-seven years. He has been a visiting professor at Princeton, Rutgers, Drew, Yale, Northwestern, and Emory universities, an Adjunct Professor at Union Theological Seminary, and he was Visiting Professor at Yale Divinity School from 2004 to 2008. He has also taught in the Columbia Graduate School of Journalism.

A prize-winning historian, Dr. Balmer is the author of more than a dozen books, including *Redeemer: The Life of Jimmy Carter* and *Bad Faith: Race and the Rise of the Religious Right*. His second book, *Mine Eyes Have Seen the Glory: A Journey into the Evangelical Subculture in America*, now in its fifth edition, was made into a three-part documentary for PBS. Dr. Balmer was nominated for an Emmy for writing and hosting that series.

His work has appeared in such venues as the *New Republic*, *Christianity Today*, *Christian Century*, *Washington Post Book World*, and the *New York Times Book Review*. His essays have been published in several anthologies, including *The Best Christian Writing 2000* and the ninth edition of the *Norton Reader*, and his commentaries on religion in America have appeared in newspapers across the country, including the *Los Angeles Times*, the *Washington Post*, the *St. Louis Post-Dispatch*, the *Philadelphia Inquirer*, the *New York Times*, the *Minneapolis Star Tribune*, the *Des Moines Register*, and the *Santa Fe New Mexican*.